MAPPING THE FUTURE

Bernardine Evaristo won the Booker Prize 2019 with her eighth book, a 'fusion fiction', *Girl, Woman, Other*. The author of novels, essays, poetry, journalism, literary criticism and drama, her memoir, *Manifesto: On Never Giving Up* was published in 2021. She has initiated many successful arts' inclusion projects and is the curator of the *Black Britain: Writing Back* book series for Penguin Random House. The recipient of many awards, including two British Book Awards, she is Professor of Creative Writing at Brunel University London and President of the Royal Society of Literature. Her first verse novel *Lara* (1997) was republished by Bloodaxe Books in 2009.

Karen McCarthy Woolf: see page 165.

Nathalie Teitler: see page 170.

MAPPING
THE
FUTURE

THE COMPLETE WORKS POETS

FOREWORD BY
BERNARDINE EVARISTO

EDITED BY
KAREN McCARTHY WOOLF
& NATHALIE TEITLER

BLOODAXE BOOKS

ISBN: 978 1 78037 671 4

First published 2023 by
Bloodaxe Books Ltd,
Eastburn,
South Park,
Hexham,
Northumberland NE46 1BS.

www.bloodaxebooks.com
For further information about Bloodaxe titles
please visit our website and join our mailing list
or write to the above address for a catalogue.

Supported using public funding by
**ARTS COUNCIL
ENGLAND**

Cover design: Neil Astley & Pamela Robertson-Pearce.

Printed in Great Britain by Bell & Bain Limited, Glasgow, Scotland, on
acid-free paper sourced from mills with FSC chain of custody certification.

CONTENTS

ROUND 1

ESSAYS

FOREWORD

It is now almost twenty years since I sat on the jury for Next Generation Poets, the decennial poetry promotion whereby 20 poets, who have published a first collection in the preceding 10 years, are selected as the most promising of their generation. It was 2004, and I discovered that out of some 120 books submitted, none were by poets of colour. I called in the five books I knew to be eligible, in spite of resistance from the organisers who didn't understand why this was an issue. I knew it was a major issue because publishers simply weren't publishing new poets of colour and nobody seemed to notice, or if they did, they didn't care. In the end, only one poet of colour made the list. Fired up to do something about this, I initiated the *Free Verse* report followed by The Complete Works mentoring scheme for poets of colour. Directed by Dr Nathalie Teitler, it ran successfully for ten years due to her exemplary commitment and solicitude in curating a wide-ranging programme for the 30 talented poets selected for it. Nathalie writes more fully about these projects in her stirring introduction.

I often explain the origins of this scheme, because this is how change happens. An individual, a collective, a community decide to improve a situation that adversely affects them or others. Through protest, setting up schemes, or lobbying, they aim to yield positive results. Change does not arise out of apathy, or when we feel immobilised by despair or pessimism, or when we all passively hope that others will take the lead, or when we adopt a laissez-faire approach, believing that society's inequalities will self-correct without our intervention. Change happens because we actively work towards it as an objective.

Today, I am so proud to see the writings of all 30 mentored poets filling the pages of this landmark anthology; and heartened to see that many more British poets of colour have emerged in recent times into a more receptive publishing climate than ever before. We're not there yet, but the developments thus far have been enormous and impactful. The projects, the lobbying, the speaking out, seems to be paying off – for now. The cumulative achievements of so many of The Complete Works poets sends messages to new writers that a career in poetry can also be for them. There are no longer a few black and Asian poets carving out careers, often seen as examples of exceptionalism, but we now have scores of poets employing the widest range of poetic styles and sensibilities, and operating at every level of the literature sector.

Furthermore, I am increasingly impressed with the quality of the poetry being published today, as well as the intellectual interrogation of ideas around poetry in the essay format. This is demonstrated so admirably in *Mapping the Future*, framed by Karen McCarthy's Woolf's brilliant and incisive preface. When I cast my mind back to the early eighties when I first began to write poetry, there really was very little available to us wannabe black and Asian British poets – no books, no support network, no guidance

Creative writing pedagogy in the UK was in its nascent stages forty years ago, only one university taught it as a subject, and as the poetry establishment was overwhelmingly white, we we didn't have access to it and there was no interest in including us. We really were worlds apart. The performance poetry scene was more accommodating to spoken word poets, typically with their origins in the Caribbean. The idea of mentorships was decades away and books on the craft of poetry tended to be either academic or proscriptive, traditional and alienating, certainly to someone such as myself.

Today's poets have structured schemes, workshops and courses available to them, and they can be inspired by the many poetry collections out there from previously overlooked communities. It is the ripple effect out to those for whom aspiration solidifies into ambition when they see that sustaining a career as a black or Asian poet feels attainable. And I am so impressed with how today's new voices confidently handle poetic forms with dexterity and negotiate the slippery semantics and possibilities of language. The level of sophistication, even in debut collections, often astounds me.

The advances that have been made since 2004, especially in the past five years alone, are noteworthy, but I am not so naive as to think that the march onwards will be free of setbacks, of formidable foes. We must never be complacent about social progress. History is a great teacher, if we know and understand it. Many of us are reminded of the rise of fascism in 1930s Europe. We cannot ignore the warnings inherent in the current geopolitical climate, such as the surge to the right, the mass brainwashing by demagogues and some of the media, the revocation of human rights, and a truly 21st-century phenomenon, the negative (as opposed to the positive) capabilities of AI to infect our lives, our societies, to distort the truth with fake everything, and even to write poems, essays, reviews, novels, plays.

As this anthology demonstrates so pertinently, poets of colour are free to write about anything they want. It's a sign of real progress, real equality. Anyone trying to lump this body of work into the 'identity' box is missing the point and imposing a critical cliché onto work that exploded out of that box a long time ago, if it was ever in it. This poetry deserves serious readings, not a critical approach based on preconceptions – mistaking fallacy for the truth. Critics need to ask themselves, 'If this poetry *isn't* about identity, then what *is* it about?' Perhaps this will begin a more interesting process of discovering the layers of meaning in the poems.

While I wish to celebrate The Complete Works poets, and the many others who have injected UK poetry with such wildly different perspectives, cultures and energies, we need to be aware that what is new today, can become outdated tomorrow. Complacency is the death of creativity. Doors that we have prised open can just as quickly be shut on us with the full force of those for whom a slightly more egalitarian culture feels like they are being discriminated against, they are the ones being persecuted, even when they continue to dominate, in real terms – as the majority of the writers, publishers, literary editors, festival directors, media owners and producers, academics and funders.

We must continue to ensure that poetry from our communities becomes embedded in our society – creatively, critically, culturally, institutionally. And while the future is ultimately unknowable, that shouldn't stop us laying the foundations for our ideal version of it.

BERNARDINE EVARISTO
London, July 2023

INTRODUCTION

Sunday 15th January 2023 at the Royal Festival Hall. It is a cold London night. Ten poets stand on a stage often occupied by international orchestras and celebrities. The event is sold out, the audience waiting eagerly. It is the reading for the T.S. Eliot Poetry Prize shortlist, one of the most prestigious events in the UK poetry calendar. In previous years, it has not been known for the diversity of the prize winners, nor the audience. But tonight is different. Four of the eight poets standing on the stage are Black.[1] Three are fellows of The Complete Works (TCW), a national development programme for Black and Asian poets, founded by literary activist Bernardine Evaristo in 2007. Tonight, their words light a fire in the audience, an audience of all ages and backgrounds. Rapt, they hang on every word as it falls into the silence.

This is history being made. This is the new face of poetry in the UK. Rewind to 2005 and the idea a night like that at the Southbank Centre could ever happen is a dream few are brave enough to imagine. This is the year the *Free Verse* report is published,[2] investigating the level of diversity in UK poetry. The figures are even worse than expected. Fewer than 1% of the poets published by major presses in the UK are Black or Asian. Evaristo, the force behind the report, decides that something must be done.

That something is a new poetry development programme for poets of colour. A programme that selects the most talented poets from a national call out, offering them mentoring, seminars, and professional development from the most well-established poets in the UK. Over time, the programme becomes something much greater: one of the most successful poetry collectives in the world.

Back in 2005 there are few mentoring programmes in UK poetry, with little understanding of what they can achieve long-term. None attempt what The Complete Works is trying to achieve. It is a leap of faith.

---

[1] Denise Saul, Victoria Adukwei Bulley, Yomi Ṣode (all TCW fellows), and Anthony Joseph, who wins the prize.

[2] Published by Spread the Word: Eds Mel Larsen, Danuta Kean.

TCW officially begins in 2007, and at its inception is run by London's literature development organisation Spread the Word co-founded by Evaristo). But it quickly becomes apparent that it needs someone to manage it. This is where my story with TCW begins.[3]

I have just completed a successful national mentoring and translation programme for Exiled Writers Ink. I have a PhD in Latin American poetry and years of working as an activist. I know little of the UK poetry world. To my surprise, I am invited to interview for the post. Years later I remember that Bernardine's unwavering gaze seemed to look straight through me. I stutter, forget who my favourite poets are. My mind goes blank. I am certain I did not get the job. But my belief in the possibility of change and community, the idea that poetry can and should be for everyone, somehow wins out. I am offered the post and begin the journey of a lifetime.

It is not easy. In the early days, I am asked outright by top figures in literature, 'Do Black and Asian poets even publish full collections?' Senior poets and editors tell me that poets of colour will never get published by major presses, but they are brave to try. And these are the ones who are supposed to be supporters of diversity, friends of TCW. There are grumbles behind my back, and sometimes to my face, from many in the literature world. They say TCW is just ticking boxes, that nothing will change.

I make mistakes. I learn from them. I learn how much I do not know. In the very early days we have a tutor, a very well-known British poet, who comes to speak to the poets in the first round of TCW, including Malika Booker, Roger Robinson and Nick Makoha – poets who will go on to win many prizes, both national and international, including the T.S. Eliot Prize. The tutor tells them that the British Empire and the history of colonialism is a thing to be celebrated. There is an awkward silence. The tutor is not invited back.

Some of the mentors try to push the poets to write in a different style, with the specific goal of getting published by the larger poetry presses. They misunderstand the aim. We are not trying

---

[3] After the first round, I was invited by Arts Council England (ACE) to run TCW as an independent organisation.

to change the poets, we are trying to change the poetry landscape. The poets, particularly those in the first cohort, are forgiving and continue to believe in the programme. They start to publish collections, win awards.

By the time of the second round of TCW, which begins in 2012, there are far more applicants. The community of poets of colour start to have faith in its vision, what it is trying to achieve. And they can see that it is succeeding. It is at this point that I add a new clause to the mentor's contracts: that they will strive to help the poets strengthen their own unique voice, rather than attempting to shape it.

The road is still not always smooth. There is a tutor, editor of a well-known poetry journal, who is asked directly by a second round TCW poet why they do not publish more Black and brown poets. The editor replies that they do not wish to "dumb down" for their readers. Some poets walk out of the session. I cannot blame them.

The grumblings from the mainstream poetry sector continue. As the TCW poets begin to win more prizes, publish more collections, this grumbling grows louder. But change cannot be stopped. In 2015, three poets from TCW – Karen McCarthy Woolf, Mona Arshi, and Sarah Howe – are shortlisted for the Forward Prize for Best First Collection. Arshi wins. And Howe's *Loop of Jade* wins that year's T.S. Eliot Prize.

A third round of TCW begins in 2017. More collections are published, more awards are won, more recognition gained. TCW poets win Forward Prizes (Will Harris), the *Sunday Times* Young Writer of the Year (Sarah Howe and Raymond Antrobus), and much more. There are almost no literature festivals or platforms that do not feature TCW poets.

There are still some in the mainstream who complain that it is temporary, that the poets do not deserve these prizes. The world seems to disagree. By 2023 the figure of Black and Asian poets published by major presses is up to 20%. TCW fellows have published over 30 collections, meaning they have made a significant contribution to this figure.

What is most exciting is the incredible diversity within their writing. The beautiful range in the style and themes of poets who write from the position of "other". Poets who write between cultures, sometimes between languages, challenging normative ideas of power, sexuality and more in a way that speaks to the world we live in today. It is this beautiful diversity that is celebrated in *Mapping the Future*, an anthology including the work of all 30 writers who've taken part in TCW over its ten-year span.

Mapping the Future offers a snapshot of the brilliance of the TCW poets, but it does not tell the whole story, particularly of the programme's long-term, continuing impact. Winning prizes is one thing, but the poets have also become significant figures shaping the UK poetry landscape. Several have completed PhDs and are now lecturing, shaping the next generations of poets, readers and critics.[4] Many have gone on to judge the prizes they were once told they could never hope to win, with Robinson serving as T.S. Eliot Prize judge, Booker and Rishi Dastidar as Forward and Costa judges, and Arshi on the panel selecting the *Sunday Times* Young Writer of the Year award.

TCW fellows are also making strides as guest editors of major journals such as *The Poetry Review* and *Magma*, and imprints – Kayo Chingonyi as editor of Bloomsbury's new poetry list. TCW fellows also take up places on boards, further influencing the landscape: Arshi (Poetry School), Makoha (Arvon), Leo Boix (*Magma*) while Dastidar serves as chair of Spread the Word for six years.

As judges, lecturers, critics and editors they are now significant figures in a sector from which they were once excluded.

The poets have also become ground-breakers in terms of challenging genres. Roger Robinson continues to combine poetry and music in his highly successful career as a much-lauded musician. Inua Ellams is a multi-award winning playwright with many sold-out plays at the National Theatre also viewed by millions online. His work, most notably, *The Half God of Rainfall*, is a combination of poetry and prose. Arshi becomes the first TCW poet to publish a novel, *Somebody Loves You*, an experimental novel that wins international acclaim and is shortlisted for the Jhalak and Goldsmiths Prize. More novels will arrive in 2024, as the poets continue to challenge the space between poetry and prose. Three books of essays will also be published, as well as many new poetry collections. Raymond Antrobus has written a ground-

---

[4] Karen McCarthy Woolf and Denise Saul have both completed their PhDs. Malika Booker and Nick Makoha are in the final stages of their doctoral studies. Sarah Howe already had a PhD on entering the programme and is a senior lecturer. All are also university and further education lecturers.

breaking children's book about a deaf/ disabled boy that has been translated into many languages. Jay Bernard won the Ted Hughes Prize for their poetry film featuring the poems in their debut collection *Surge*. Yomi Ṣode is combining theatre and poetry in new ways, as well as working closely with Chineke! Orchestra to produce a seminal piece of work with composer James B. Wilson at Southbank Centre inspired by an iconic moment in the Black Live Matters protests in the UK. He and McCarthy Woolf have also worked closely with visual artists, created poetry films and continue to expand the range of what poetry can do. British Latinx poet Boix has won numerous translation prizes, including a PEN Translates Award, and has brought many new Latinx poets to the attention of an English-language audience. His bilingual poetry has played a role in challenging the idea that poetry in the UK must be almost entirely in English – something that he had to fight hard to achieve, with early tutors suggesting that he might wish to simply write in Spanish.

TCW fellows have also taken up the fundamental work of the programme, nurturing and developing poets of colour. Makoha has set up the Obsidian Foundation, for Black poets in the UK. Based on the US organisation Cave Canem, of which he is a fellow (along with Booker and Antrobus), it has already become an important feature of the poetry landscape. Howe, in partnership with poet Sandeep Parmar, founded Ledbury Critics, an organisation that has helped to develop the writing and pub-lication of over 30 poetry critics of colour. This has played a key role in ensuring that collections by Black and Asian poets are reviewed in the national press (they were previously largely ignored), and that the critiques are meaningful and nuanced. The Ledbury Critics cohort are now regular reviewers for the *Telegraph*, *Financial Times* and more.

I have been fortunate to be able to continue this legacy by helping Bloodaxe to set up the wonderful James Berry Poetry Prize, an initiative devised with Evaristo. This offers three poets per round (every three years) the opportunity to be mentored and have a full collection published by the UK's most inclusive poetry publisher. In 2020 I also founded The Bridge, an online international collective for global majority poets, who are offered free monthly Masterclasses by some of the best Black, Asian and Latinx poets in the world.

The poetry world has also changed significantly since the start of TCW in 2007. There are new independent publishers like Broken Sleep, Out-Spoken and Penned in the Margins expanding the range of what is brought to British audiences. This is not to overlook other independent publishers, most notably flipped eye and Peepal Tree, founded before TCW – along with Bloodaxe and Carcanet – which have made a huge impact on both the poets and the wider landscape. The poetry lists of trade publishers which had previously included very few or no poets of colour saw a complete reversal, most notably at Chatto and Penguin. Granta took on Will Harris and Jonathan Cape outbid four other publishers to acquire Momtaza Mehri's debut collection. And there are many more mentoring and development schemes, including the excellent Women's Prize (run by the Rebecca Swift Foundation and managed by The Literary Consultancy).

Poetry in the UK is constantly changing and developing, becoming more multilingual as it reflects the diversity of Britain: over 300 languages are spoken in London alone. There are more links with the United States and a global audience. I am certain that there are many new developments to come, particularly in areas such as poetry film, cross-arts work and experimental fiction. I know that The Complete Works fellows will play a large part in bringing about this future, and that their legacy is one that continues to grow.

I would like to finish by thanking Bloodaxe for publishing all three TCW anthologies over the years, and for Neil Astley's faith in it from the beginning. I would also like to thank Bernardine Evaristo for founding TCW and doing so much important work in the area of literary activism. I would also like to thank the TCW poets for their faith in me. Most of all, I would like to thank you, the audience and readers – you are the ones who keep the flame of poetry alive by buying our books and attending our readings.

NATHALIE TEITLER

PREFACE

Poems as a Form of Knowledge Production

The title of this Preface (mis)quotes Victoria Adukwei Bulley, who writes that 'dreaming is a form of knowledge production' in her poem of the same name. It is a compelling sentiment, as well as an idea, and one which speaks eloquently to this current gathering.

Mapping the Future includes all thirty Fellows of The Complete Works mentoring programme and with them it captures multiple geographies, cultures, identities and modes of practice and poetics over a fifteen-year period. The landscape which it set out to transform has altered radically, not only within literature, but throughout the arts, and the publishing sector. Both Nathalie Teitler and Bernardine Evaristo speak to these dramatic shifts in demographics and relate some of the combined literary achievements across all three intakes, which comprise poets of the Middle Eastern, African, Caribbean, Asian and American diasporas.

This book is organised alphabetically via cohort. It includes essays on process and poetics as well as poems, starting from the most recent round in 2017 back to the initial intake, which I was a part of, in 2008, when, as stated, UK poetry was statistically whiter and far less porous to othered poetries than it is today. Returning now to the entirety of the Fellowship in 2023, the fact that the UK has been through seismic political change in that period is discernible. The nation where we make our homes and into which we release our poetry is post-Brexit and post-pandemic. The rhetoric, narrative and language these occurrences produced as political events have brought us to a place where exceptionalist nostalgia reigns over reality; a country in the grip of a collective (un)consciousness which Rishi Dastidar describes so aptly in his satirical poem 'The Brexit Book of the Dead' as 'Empire 2.0'.

Beyond these vital matters of representation and identity, the idea that poems (and with them imaginative material that exists beyond Cartesian logic) might exist as acts of transformation and decoloniality is powerful. Keats' negative capability captures that sense of writing into the unknown, but the canon and its environs are complicated for black, brown and non-white writers whose collective cultural knowledge systems have been historically undermined. Inevitably, writing into such spaces is also to write against them under what we might broadly term a poetics of resistance. That resistance may be explicit and subtle at the same time, as in Kayo Chingonyi's poem 'Kumukanda', which expresses the ambivalent alienation of being an uninitiated boy who leaves Zambia for the UK and how this experience impacts his sense of self and language. It may be unerringly and inescapably direct, as is Warsan Shire's now iconic poem 'Home', which reminds us that in the current migratory paradigm 'no one leaves home unless home is the mouth of a shark.' It may engage with archives and/or events, as does Jay Bernard in their poem 'Clearing' which uses first person account to bring us back to the horror of the New Cross fire; a tragedy which is amplified and echoed in Roger Robinson's 'The Missing', dedicated to the victims of Grenfell. Or it may be fuelled by a focused interiority, as in Edward Doegar's 'The English Lyric', which in its quiet study of '[…]English rain / Rain I have known all my life' pushes at the illusory seams of nation-based constructs of belonging.

For the writer of colour belonging is prismatic and contingent on the relationships between community, alterity and individuality. Who we write for, what we write about and why we write it are all held within this sphere. Identity, as assigned or asserted, is present even in its absence. Momtaza Mehri captures this paradox in her compelling discussion on the benefits and drawbacks of solitude 'An Emptying, A Gathering', which explores a poetics of 'radical narcissism' where 'the margins shouldn't have to perform for the centre'. This position of decentred anti-performativity is evidenced further in the queer poetics of Bernard and via Nick Makoha's transformation of his experience as a Ugandan/British writer in exile to a community-driven manifesto in his essay 'The Black Metic'. Here he repositions the outsider at the heart of a new diasporic literature – a thread he continues to weave in a sequence of ekphrastic poems that bring the artist Jean-Michel Basquiat and a black Icarus into the frame. Yomi Ṣode also writes into spaces of visual representation, spectacle and black masculinity in painting and on film in his poem 'Exhibition 2.0'; while his evocatively titled

'An Ode to Bruv, Ting, Fam and, on Occasion, Cuz & My Man' celebrates 'How dextrous a language' slang can be; a dexterity Adam Lowe also identifies in his poem 'Elegy for the Latter-Day Teen Wilderness Years': 'We had a cribbed language others didn't understand,' he writes, 'and that gave us power.'

Leo Boix speaks to this power as possibility over deep time and from a Latinx perspective in his essay 'Multilingual Writing and Translation: A Poetics of Resistance'. As a poet and translator, Boix contests English as hegemonic default, referring the reader instead to the many indigenous languages which mix with Spanish and its dialects. Spanish is the language Shazea Quraishi also works in, and Susana Chavez Castillo's 'In the branches of your voice' is the only translation featured here, with the Spanish original included. Boix uses brief Spanish phrases sparely in his playfully rhymed 'Latin American Sonnets', but they are perfect demonstrations of how we render the mesh and blur of place. Jennifer Lee Tsai's moving lyric essay 'About Chinese Women' also draws on the capacities and deficits of language in her incantatory account of her hakka heritage and her grandmother's suicide.

The sonnet is the vehicle through which Malika Booker enacts an intersectional feminist reversioning of the stories and fables which populate the King James Bible. 'My Ghost in the Witness Box' and its associated essay are demonstration and explication of the Bible's role in a creolised Caribbean vernacular, which patterns not only everyday speech in the region but also its moral and ethical temperature, particularly with regard to the lives (and deaths) of women. Booker's poetics of resistance is a moment of literal witness in which she deploys patterns of repetition to elevate the conceit of legal testimony to high lyric.

When witness steps outside of the courtroom we discover new poetries of nature and ecology. Ian Humphrey's 'Swifts and the Awakening City' adopts a hybrid form, namely a Haibun punctuated by outbreaks of concrete poetry in lieu of the haiku, that moves fluidly so as to approximate the flight of the endangered swift. Raymond Antrobus gives account of his relationship with the rural, with green spaces and parks, as a London, and specifically Hackney, native. His essay 'Bird Song and Resonance' follows his journey, from the UK to Oklahoma City, which he notes was also home to Ralph Ellison, where he lived with his wife over lockdown. For Antrobus, who is deaf, it was necessary to use his hearing aid to hear the birdsong which lifted his spirits in difficult times. His relationship with sound plays out elsewhere in the formal innovation of the poem 'Horror Scene as Black English Royal (Captioned)' which uses the subtitle/caption as lyric soundtrack. Another writer who reflects explicitly on the impact of the pandemic is Mona Arshi, who like Mehri, also considers the effects of solitude and isolation. In lyrically intense poems and expansive prose she draws our gaze inwards to a mesmeric reckoning of the self and the soul, to moments of pause, to a quiet, steady and cumulative attention – a characteristic we encounter elsewhere, and notably in the works of Denise Saul, Will Harris and Sarah Howe.

Throughout the anthology linguistic and formal experimentation are various and at times play out via strategies of embodiment: Inua Ellam's crisply rhymed tercets are mimetic of the pitter-patter of basketball which the poem's characters play together in this extract from the dramatic fable *The Half God of Rainfall* while Eileen Pun draws on her background in martial arts and choreography in 'Longways / Crosswise' a poetry & dance sequence defining the Morecambe Bay passages'. My contribution here is also hybrid and utilises the *zuihitsu* as means by which to think about the idea of diaspora poetics as both a scattering and a drawing together.

There is of course no singular knowledge 'output' from this remarkable body of work, it would be reductive to imagine there might be. *Mapping the Future* carries in its aura poetry's dreamlike ephemera underpinned by imaginative structure and linguistic precision. In his essay, 'Bad Dreams' Will Harris shrugs off the impositions of race as a construct which felt like 'being possessed by other people's dreams' in favour of poetry, as a genre in which 'reality could be freely altered or made anew'. It is perhaps this transformative quality that is the most frequent visitor in this assembly, sometimes experienced as desire, that beacon of the future, and at others in the immediacy of the present moment.

Finally, it is important to note that *Mapping the Future* is different to other anthologies because of its collegiate qualities. The Complete Works was a mentoring programme first and foremost, where the tradition of handing down intergenerational knowledge was formalised in order to make that process inclusive. Its reach was not confined to the thirty poets selected and represented here: its overarching ideal was one of the extended family. So many poets were generous with their time and wisdom, as mentors, advocates and associates; so many helped lay a path on a bridge across waters they'd been forced to swim. Poetry is not a luxury, this we know; but the opportunity to develop and refine a practice, to hone our craft, to receive advice on how to navigate an uncertain industry, to have a safe space in which to formulate and articulate individual and shared poetics that embrace multiple realities is rare. For this I think I can speak for all when I say we are truly thankful.

KAREN McCARTHY WOOLF`

22

ROUND 1

RAYMOND ANTROBUS

Raymond Antrobus, FRSL MBE, was born in Hackney, London, to an English mother and Jamaican father. He is the author of *To Sweeten Bitter* (Out-Spoken Press, 2017), *The Perseverance* (Penned in the Margins / Tin House, 2018), *All the Names Given* (Picador / Tin House, 2021), and two children's picture books, *Can Bears Ski?* (Walker Books, 2020) and *Terrible Horses* (Walker Books, 2024). . In 2019 he became the first ever poet to be awarded the Rathbones Folio Prize, for best work of literature in any genre. Other accolades include the Ted Hughes Award, the Lucille Clifton Legacy Award, Poetry Book Society Choice, *Sunday Times* Young Writer of the Year Award and *The Guardian* Poetry Book of the Year 2018, as well as being shortlisted for the Griffin Prize and Forward Prize. In 2018 he was awarded the Geoffrey Dearmer Prize (judged by Ocean Vuong) for his poem 'Sound Machine'. A selection of his poems were added to the GCSE syllabus in 2022. *All the Names Given* was shortlisted for the Costa Poetry Award and the T.S Eliot Prize.

The Perseverance

Love is the man overstanding

PETER TOSH

I wait outside THE PERSEVERANCE.
Just poppin in here for a minute.
I'd heard him say it many times before
like all kids with a drinking father,
watch him disappear
into smoke and laughter.

There is no such thing as too much laughter,
My father says, drinking in THE PERSEVERANCE
until everything disappears —
I'm outside counting minutes,
waiting for the man, my *father*
to finish his shot and take me home before

it gets dark. We've been here before,
no such thing as too much laughter
unless you're my mother without my father,
working weekends while THE PERSEVERANCE
spits him out for a minute.
He gives me 50p to make me disappear.

50p in my hand, I disappear
like a coin in a parking meter before
the time runs out. How many minutes
will I lose listening to the laughter
spilling from THE PERSEVERANCE
while strangers ask, *where is your father?*

I stare at the doors and say, *my father
is working.* Strangers who don't disappear
but hug me for my perseverance.
Dad said *this will be the last time* before,
while the TV spilled canned laughter,
us, on the sofa in his council flat, knowing any minute

25

the yams will boil, any minute,
I will eat again with my father,
who cooks and serves laughter
good as any Jamaican who disappeared
from the Island I tasted before
overstanding our heat and perseverance.

I still hear *popping in for a minute*, see him disappear.
We lose our fathers before we know it.
I am still outside THE PERSEVERANCE, listening for the laughter.

Horror Scene as Black English Royal (Captioned)

One night, in the shower, you look at your hands and they are your great-great-great grandfather's owner's hands. They are leaning on the walls of his boiling house

[sound of camp fires]

Your feet are the whitest sugar and you don't know where to step or what you're really holding when you speak into your Grandmother's bedroom, her jewels hanging by the mirror

[sound of secret room]

Is all of this what your great-great-great-Grandfather would have thrown you overboard for? Does it matter? Does your blood have to make all this old centurion noise?

[sound of fractures]

You won't strain to hear who or what is at the bottom of the ocean. What ship will turn, sink, rot, burn, your mouth when you speak your reparation receipts?

[sound of sinking]

Your tongue tasting the iron bit, the River Nile, the Gulf Coast, the Thames, the Abeng horn. When you cry, what rhythm, the crown? What is this sound, erupting from the whitest black blood in the land?

LEO BOIX

Leo Boix is a bilingual Latinx poet born in Argentina who lives and works in London and Deal, Kent. His debut English collection *Ballad of a Happy Immigrant* (Chatto & Windus, 2021) was awarded the Poetry Book Society Wild Card Choice. Boix has been included in many anthologies, such as *Ten: Poets of the New Generation* (Bloodaxe Books), *The Best New British and Irish Poets Anthology 2019-2020* (Black Spring Press), *Islands Are But Mountains: Contemporary Poetry from Great Britain* (Platypus Press), *100 Poems to Save the Earth* (Seren Books), *100 Queer Poems* (Vintage/Penguin) and *Un Nuevo Sol: British Latinx Writers* (flipped eye), among others. He is co-director of *Un Nuevo Sol*, a scheme to nurture new voices of Latinx writers in the UK, an advisory board member of the Poetry Translation Centre, and a board member of *Magma* Poetry. He has written poems commissioned by Royal Kew Gardens, the National Poetry Library, Whitstable Biennale, Bradford Literary Festival, Estuary Festival, La Linea Festival and the Kent Mining Museum in England. He was the recipient of the Bart Wolffe Poetry Prize, the Keats-Shelley Prize, a PEN Award, and The Society of Authors' Foundation and K. Blundell Trust.

A Latin American Sonnet

There is a palm tree somewhere, and a bird
of paradise that speaks to me in my dreams.
Well, not actually a bird, more like a blurred
vision of a plane crossing the endless seams
of a continent too big to fit here, in this isle
of gold where we plant elder for shade, sit
under a dusty sun, whatever it takes. Miles

away from everywhere, in my dreams a Brit
asks all the questions, and I often reply: who-
ever comes for tea will one day have to leave
for a better world. I end up kissing the beau
who is from here, or just about, so naive!
A blue parrot repeats my name in old English,
Leo, Leonardo. Perhaps it was a dream, well...*ish*.

A Latin American Sonnet III

We are the only Latin Americans in Deal;
there was a loud Uruguayan lady who left
for Madrid and was never seen again. I feel
like a parakeet sometimes, I have to confess.
I have a boyfriend now who, like me, came
from Buenos Aires. He has lived here almost
all his life, people can't tell till he says his name.
Our old house is a pseudo-Argentine outpost
where we drink hot maté, eat steaks, inside here
we speak an odd Spanish, a mismatch melee
of words we've created: *mono-pato, a dormir*,
as if we were in our own world, both castaways.
Sometimes it's tough and sometimes it gets better,
Let's drink to that and to our long life together.

Eucalyptus

After years of searching
        I find my father standing
by the old tree he'd pruned
        every spring to grow leafy
before the sweltering heat
        of our subtropical Summer.
Who's there? he asks.
        I'm your son, dad. *Tu hijo.*
Your first wife's dead,
        like you. We buried her
south of Buenos Aires. *Y yo?*,
        he enquires. A dirty maté gourd
in his tarred hands. You're
        interred somewhere north
of the General Paz motorway.
        He nods, sips his sweet drink,
gives me a tangerine, then
        crosses the empty patio
to his unkempt toolshed,
        handsaws, nails getting rustier.
I leave by the yard door,
        he whistles from his world
        through the dream
        where the tree grows taller
every time I look back.

OMIKEMI NATACHA BRYAN

Omikemi is a writer, creative mentor, somatics facilitator and ritual keeper and engage these practices to create spaces for alongsideness and listening. *Their Grief Ritual Practice, Crossings*, is forthcoming in facilitators guide, *How We Hold*, for Serpentine Galleries. They currently work facilitating somatics as part of The Heartwood, a black and global majority body work projected they created in 2021 and for Disability Arts Online as a freelance writer, creative mentor and more recently as editor for *Onyx*, a collective and publication exploring (dis)ability and racism. They are currently working on *Landmarks*, memoir and ritual performance exploring home making, leaving and belonging.

Sirens

(for Nila Gupta)

The friend tells me no one knows what happened.
          The call ends, I keep the phone against my ear

straining for more words—words that would

          make it make sense. I'm reminded of a poet
living in New York who said he could have stood

          on the sidewalk to watch the towers fall but decided

on a bank of televisions instead, in the hope of words
          that would make it make sense. It's three days

          after my first shift at the suicide respite place,
I feel like a heart surgeon who does a good enough job

most days but on this day comes home to find
          a close relative dead from a cardiac arrest.

Days later, I'm listening to a conversation between the artist
          Sia and Gabor Mate. The artist says
I thought the feelings would kill me and I'm irate

          that for now she has found a way to live in a house
that once threatened to burn her down.
                    I want to tell her

          sometimes they do, the feelings, they kill you.

But of course, this statement isn't entirely true, in the way
          that when you ask a kid what colour water is
they will likely say blue.

          I think of all the fires, ones that never
caught the grasses, the ones we wanted to start but never did.

32

No one knows is a statement that isn't entirely true.

> Some of our sirens are the scars
> you wanted me to believe were stretchmarks.

Many of our sirens are mostly silent
> and take years for others to learn their distinct pitch.

I'm told no one knows what happened
> but some of us know   how we get talked into thinking

> the wand of light on water is a bridge —

Home

I wanted to write about belonging, the smell of *All Purpose*
seasoning, mixed with lavender air freshener and steamed fish.
I wanted to write about cold evenings in steel boxes
talking with strangers whose voices felt and sounded like tissue paper.
I wanted to write about Maggie coming down from the house
in her nightgown, telling the men reading each other's hands
— *hush you mout or cum out*. I wanted to write about the hours
at hospitals, sitting on perforated metal chairs more suited to stadiums
than a place of care. About the front room with the glass fish
in the cabinets and plastic covers on the seats, —for guests only.
About the police, the police bringing you into the front room
after one of your shoplifting sprees. About the six-week holidays
with cousins Dun Dun, Denny and Ackee, and the threat
of sudden violence somehow still being reassuring to me.
About the home carried inside, concocted of adrenaline, cortisol
and epinephrine. About him steering his way back at 3am
slurring around like a lone pinball in a machine. No, like flies
skating, falling, skating and falling down the egg white
of some dead creature's eyes while we pretended to sleep.

VICTORIA ADUKWEI BULLEY

Victoria Adukwei Bulley's work has appeared widely in publications including *The White Review*, *The London Review of Books* and *The Atlantic*. She is the winner of an Eric Gregory Award, and her critically acclaimed debut collection, *Quiet*, won both the Rathbones Folio Prize for Poetry and the John Pollard Foundation International Poetry Prize, and was shortlisted for the T.S. Eliot Prize. *Quiet* was published by Faber & Faber in the UK and in North America by Knopf in 2022.

Declaration

if sickness begins in the gut, if

      I live in the belly of the beast, if

here at the heart of empire –

      if careful in the house of the host, if

      quiet at the hearth of the host, if

here at the home of empire –

      if I live in the belly of the beast,

let me beget sickness in its gut.

Pandemic vs Black Folk

It never was a virus that came for us, not really.
Don't ask me what my mother knows about that.
If yours never told you, perhaps we can't be friends.
We always were too welcoming a people, or so it's said,
or should I say, *peoples*. Plural as the distance between leaf
& leaves; as the difference between twig & tree – what we were
before being rolled into singular, brought to the flame & lit
for an inhale that hasn't ended. Who are *your* peoples?
If we need to know, we'll ask who sent you. If you're suspect,
we'll ask where you're *really* from. If you're safe, we'll bring water
on a tray, say: *sit down, wash your hands, eat*. It never was a virus
that killed us, no, not even if it killed en masse. Worse things
have happened at sea, or so it goes. & if anybody knows that, we do.

Suddenly, all across the land, this great land,
this dunya, this Great Britain, this Britain First,
this Brexit means Brexit so fresh & so green
green & pleasant land, it seems there is no toilet roll,
no soap. As if the Moors came & snatched it back,
astaghfirullah. Shelves good as new – empty as the day
they were built. Meanwhile, in the tinned food aisle, nary
a tin of tomatoes to be found. I guess it's good folks
are learning how to cook. A prayer for our elders, who
only stepped out for fresh air. There's rice at home yet
for the time being. As for toilet paper, that's a different thing.
If cleanliness were godliness all along, no Columbus could have
made the New World new. If cleanliness were godliness, really,
there would be soap in the shops even now.

Things being still early, we hug first & remember second.
Arms are thrown about backs, fingers gesture towards
hair, admiring a careful day's work of braids.
Cue laughter as usual, cue knowing smiles –
& what is it that we feel, beneath all this, that gives
our meetings their sugared ease? Not denial, quite.
Not humour to evade dissemblance this time.
The body keeps a logbook of what happens to it.
Bones can speak long after the flesh has gone. Often,
on the train, the one seat that's free is the one
that's next to me & that's just fine. You know a girl
likes a space to place her bag. Maybe social distancing
is another way of saying that. Yes. *When I walk into a room
I never know what I might do.* In this skin, sis, I'm a virus too.

Dreaming Is a Form of Knowledge Production

Nobody's immune to their ego taking the wheel.
Dreaming is a form of knowledge production
& they don't want it to be that easy for us.
As in: lay your head on a pillow

                             wake up holding
something new. I said what I said, not what you say
I said. Pigs are outside the house, but next door
this time. It's not something our relationship
will be able to survive. He doesn't show it, the cat,
but he loves me so. He has the gene but it hasn't
kicked in yet. Another thousand years. All thinking
& no feeling. Shut up about Freud.

WILL HARRIS

Will Harris is a London-based writer. He is the author of the poetry books *RENDANG* (2020) and *Brother Poem* (2023), both published by Granta in the UK and by Wesleyan University Press in the US. He has been shortlisted for the T.S. Eliot Prize and won the Forward Prize for Best First Collection. He helps facilitate the Southbank New Poets Collective with Vanessa Kisuule, and co-translated Habib Tengour's *Consolatio* with Delaina Haslam in 2022. He is currently a Visiting Poetry Fellow at UEA working towards a community-led archive of poets' work

*　　*　　*

In June, outrageous stood the flagons on
the pavement which extended to the river
where we spoke of everything except
the fear that would, when habit ended, be
depended on. Our fear of darkness as
the fear of darkness never ending. To
hell with it, you said, and why not? Let's buy
a dirty and slobbery farm in Albion. What
country is this? There was the big loom
we little mice were born to tarry in.
Its patter made the bad things better. O
we sang against the light as we sang
against the battens! Cold that June and mist-
shapen, the river mind and all else matter,
I called you. Where are you? It's getting
dark. But these being statements, they ran
away before I could say *hummock coastline theft*.
This is where we used to speak of everything.
I need one more hour please. One more
hour. My affordable memories sold, I hung
my phone from the highest flagpole and kissed
the face of England once discreetly, though
it wasn't you and neither was the mist
wherefrom in dingle darkness buzzed a single
notification. Call me when you get this.
And see I'm calling now, whether or not
this is *now* or *in time*.

Seven Dreams of Richard Spencer

1

Once I woke up with the actual gilded horns
of a cuck and you admired them and assured me
I need not fear dreams that pass through the horned
gates, but then I turned into a yellow cowfish,
flopping on the bed, and you picked me up
by my small horns and flushed me down the toilet.

2

Once I believed myself to be a cuckoo when, in fact,
I was a pair of binoculars looking at a cuckoo. I hung
around your neck, swaying on the drive home, where
you left me on the seat. There, I turned into a mote
of dust. The next day you sat in silence – the churring
call of a nightjar outside – while I nested in your eye.

3

Once I was a cucumber and you pretended I was
useful, but when I said I was a *Gurke* – speaking
German fluently – you tried to pickle me.
I remember wanting to turn into a kitten or
something cute but ended up as a novelty
keychain for a real estate broker called *Big Dick's*.

4

Once I was the chlorine in a public swimming
pool and I flowed into the open gills of a woman
I believed to be my mother, before it occurred
to me that my mother isn't young and doesn't have
gills. I turned into a macrophage and was able
to see that the woman I believed to be my mother
was addled with cancer, so I started to eat my way
through every cell I came across. Not because
I wanted to save her, but because it tasted good.

5

Once Europe was a market square and though
it wasn't market day I had come to sit and drink
hot chocolate and listen to the buskers, one of
whom was singing Schumann's *Dichterliebe*, which
for some reason you thought was *Bleeding Love*.
It's not, I said, but later I heard Leona Lewis's
voice in the flapping of the pigeons outside
the National Museum. The exhibits, on loan,
had been replaced by photographs. Each time
I tried to touch one, it moved. *You better back
the fuck off*, said the security guard. I turned
into a boy and girl who had lost their parents
and we hugged each other, crying.

6

Once the rain fell in vertical girders and I thought
I could walk between them, pressing my cheek
against their cold surface, but a mansion rose
about me several floors high and a voice called
telling me to leave. *Father*, I said, *why have you
forsaken me?* I turned into a great eyeball and
still he looked away, so I turned into a frog
and slipped without a sound into a millpond.

7

Once I was not myself or another man or either of
their lips exactly but the expression of a kiss they shared
and, at first, I have to say it was beautiful, but then
I felt myself turning into – or, no, recognising
myself as – a desert flower, which was even better.

Scene Change

A row of Georgian
houses slopes
down to a meadow

filled with pretty
little meadow
flowers where

you could forget
these rolling
barrows started

life as stacks of
corpses piled
high with earth

and stone that
rotted back into
the land and

only after several
generations'
growth grew

to resemble
what you might
call scenic

*

Built by the Dutch
in the century
before last

I climb the high
steps of the
bell tower and

taking in my
hands the tongue
the clapper

ring too slowly
at first aware
of my imposture

and then too
quickly in a bid
to compensate

as it dings hollow
across the
square and down

across the car
polluted outskirts
of the colony

*   *   *

Take the origin of banal: a
 bannal-mill where tenants
  carried their corn to be ground
   for the benefit of the lord. But
    imagine it without the lord, all
     of us taking our corn to the mill
      saying I'm sad, I'm lonely,
       I can't take it, and then grinding
        the corn, baking it, sharing it.
        I eat if you eat. Maybe it's the
         knowledge of what's shared –
          or could be – that stops me on
           the point of exposure, of breaking
            down, because I can't let go of
             feelings, of the belief in a singular
              self without which I disappear,
               or hear you speaking with my
                mouth, my pain in yours. Why
                 do you write? I saw you standing
                  on the corner with a bag of food.
                   When the lights changed it was
                    summer and we were by the river,
                     talking. I was trying to explain why
                      writing is pointless, but you were there.

The point of writing is to address
you. It's so embarrassing to
talk like this. At the checkout
I forgot what I had to buy.
Another memory appeared like
washing-up liquid replaced by
fizzy drinks, a feeling that didn't
begin with me. And I pictured
you saying this to yourself as
you waited on the corner with
a bag of food, also having
forgotten some obvious thing, its
place taken by the image of
a river green with scum, fish
floating to the surface in a sudden
trance. You couldn't work out
where it was or who was talking
but the fact it happened made us
both feel calm. So we decided,
standing there, to regard all
our feelings as mutual, the only
action as collective, and speech
a way of taking it to you.

IAN HUMPHREYS

Ian Humphreys is Writer in Residence at the Brontë Parsonage Museum (2023-24). His debut poetry collection *Zebra* (Nine Arches Press, 2019) was nominated for the Portico Prize. His second collection, *Tormentil* (Nine Arches, 2023), won a Royal Society of Literature 'Literature Matters' Award while in progress. He is the editor of *Why I Write Poetry* (Nine Arches), and the producer and co-editor of *After Sylvia: Poems and Essays in Celebration of Sylvia Plath* (Nine Arches). He is widely published in journals and has written for the BBC.

The grasshopper warbler's song

the singing will never be done

SIEGFRIED SASSOON

rising and falling
cool seeds of springtime
hidden in the long grass
notes balanced
on swaying stems
mirroring
the viola flow
      of bristled leg against wing
rising and falling
no melody
      just
      air decanted
      just
     how light through cloud might sound
following our footsteps like green shadows
rising and falling
rousing as a chorus
soft as salah

and the grass and the trees and the sky

Swifts and the Awakening City

my electronic friend tells me about the swifts | how they're doomed to fly
for seasons without landing | how their devilish screams mourn lost souls |
he says a god took away their feet as punishment to make them graceless
on earth | I watch them from my bedroom window | wheeling up there
near the cloud plumes | acrobats every one | swoop and catch | dive and
pincer | I've read they stab at insects with their needle beaks | tiny spiders
riding the wind on wisps of web | slurped like noodles | the friend in my
dreams says swifts mate on the wing | the tender ache of angels | why
would they want to come down here?

look down there
      cry the swifts
          really look
                  down there at Greatheed Road
                        long   and oh so winding
                                  see   how it wends its way
                            back through the centuries
                to the sugar plantations
       of St Kitts
      then on past Guy's Cliffe House
and its caves
      carved with African faces
             who were they?

my electronic friend tells me indoors is delicious | proffers soft pillows |
flock wallpaper and underfloor heating | he advises swifts never land as
the trees they roost in no longer exist | there's a dead elm in the park
across the dual carriageway | in a high wind it's an old man beckoning

                                      rest your ear
                              against cool bark
                    and you'll hear   growth
                the crack of potential
              the spine of a great novel
        snapped   kindling stretching
     over flame   listen
to the choral song

              of oaks
                     elders murmuring scripture
                          the whistle of willows
                               a kettle calling you home and then
                                         there's the monkey puzzle tree
                                                  chittering tongue-in-cheek
                                                       hace mucho frio
                                                   ¿dónde está el sol
                               where is the sun?

the friend in my dreams reminds me 120 languages are spoken in this city |
she says the swifts fly here from Africa each year | then charcoals their
arced silhouettes against Saharan skies | she draws Usman too | the soft-
spoken barber I used to visit once a month by the music museum | he'd
hum and cradle my head as he worked | no one's held me like that since I
don't know | I don't know

                          wake
                    blink
               at an open window
                          a single smoky brown feather
                               drifts
                               down
                          from the ceiling

my electronic friend tells me the swifts are local | he says they spend a
long winter submerged in mud pools by Molands Mere | reappear each
May spitting dirt | later I imagine stepping through the phony bookcase
filled with real books | I saw it in a black and white whodunnit | it pivots
and swings into other rooms | with other voices

my electronic friend tells me I'm safe indoors | far from swifts | far from
unpredictable others | far from the origami hare in the woods | Barry in
the pound bakers near Ball Hill | Sue and Geeta down Bannerbrook chip
shop | I smile at him | get comfy in the chair by the radiator | later with
the friend in my dreams I hatch a secret among the swifts | we speak
Feather | tomorrow I will fly | higher than the new student blocks on
Fairfax Street | right into the sun's stare | strong again

like a bird
with fire in its filigree heart

risen from the dust
of a sheltering city

The wood warbler's song

It's unmistakable,
a thin coin spinning on a plate.

The sound springs from nowhere
then somewhere over there.

Tangling itself round a thorn,
rising sharply through rusted bracken.

I pause until the high-pitched trill
stutters to a halt.

Heads
or tails?

It could go either way, the ICU doctor
warned us last night. And now I wonder

what news of her waits for me
down there in the valley

where my *no signal* phone
will chirp back to life in my hand.

MOMTAZA MEHRI

Momtaza Mehri is a poet and independent researcher working across criticism, translation, anti-disciplinary research practices, education, and radio. She is a former Young People's Poet Laureate for London and Frontier-Antioch Fellow at Antioch University (Los Angeles). She has also completed residencies at St Paul's Cathedral and the British Library. Her debut collection *Bad Diaspora Poems* (Jonathan Cape, 2023) is shortlisted for the Forward Prize for Best First Collection.

Fledglings

attempt (one)

A coin toss. Two birds. Two tides of acclimation. Two heads. Two kinds of newcomers. One hurtles, encased in high-strength aluminium. A suitcase stuffed with advantages. Joins the rest. Old dogs & older tricks. Empty-handed, though sleeves often reveal comfy beginnings. This group bleeds redemption. Spells out a five-year plan at the intermediate level English class. They are the spangled success story. Spit-shined exceptions. They dribble lighter fluid and ambition. They will earn their wings. Earn their keep in bleached suburbs, in fist-sized towns & strip mall sprawls. Their children will blame them for all the wrong reasons. For not passing on a mythology of lack. For throwing them down the bottomless well of aspiration. Some will call them models. Some will call them mannequins. Like their new neighbours, they will have trouble sleeping.

attempt (redux)

Two birds. One in the bush. Is bush. Fresh off the boat. Never docking. Never quite landing. Sunny-side up. They inherit a lifetime of perpetual crisis management. Movement is fractal, maddeningly lateral. Their survival is a muzzled conspiracy. Their dying is a muzzled conspiracy. They will disappoint their children. Their taste in china will always be gauche. They are workers of no distinction, of no ascendant direction. Fixed stars by which the rest of us may determine our own positions. Their accents will always be charmless. They possess an intimate knowledge of the nation's sudden bowel movements. They are possessed. Like seers, they will not be believed. Occupying the lower rungs of citizenship's mercurial ladder, they rinse shit from bed sheets, warm the hands of elders, wipe spittle as it collects at the corners of gasping mouths. They ferry the heart-broken to & from weekend vigils. Prod squealing pigs with stun guns. Return the departed to the wet earth.

One bird knows its nest better than the other.
    One bird soars & another shivers in your hands.

I AM BRINGING THE HISTORY OF THE KITCHEN SINK
INTO OUR BEDROOM AND YOU CAN'T STOP ME

Half-watching. Half-asleep. I flutter with misrecognition.
We don't ask for life, we have it thrust upon us. Young woman turns back.
Laptop glow frames an empire's rain-drenched cul-de-sac.
We don't ask for history, but it asks too much of us.
Don't want to be a mother, she says. Don't want to be a woman.
Don't want to be this particular person living this particular moment
in this forgotten corner of this dangerously particular country.
Perception is a gilded cage. I mouth along to the film, taste its pallor
like sherbet under a trained tongue. *You need someone to love you*
while you're looking for someone to love. Is there no end to this looking?
To this being looked at? And who among us hasn't mistaken a field of
        fallen soldiers
for something other than a wasteland of promises?
The fear is: the chalk of our origins will not smudge.
The fear is: it was never real but we will spend our lives pretending it was.
We will call this the purest form of love. We will call it nation.
When we say we want no part of it, we mean we want everything.
We want more than we will ever be given. The rest is history, is fossilised
        heirlooms,
is bastilles of bone and beauty, is cubicles of inherited shame, is domestic
entrapments where we build solitary shrines to our suffering.
Take this toothed necklace I refuse to pass on.

Winged, white-headed bestower of neck strains and dehydrated guilt,
hug my shivering shoulders.
My hanging albatross, my child of al-gattas, Arabic's guttural diver,
by way of Portuguese sailing ships, those carceral caravels
scouting African coasts, generously giving their name to Alcatraz,
to prisons on islands, to islands made prisons. Arm-in-arm,
two friends light my screen, walk through a twentieth-century mist,
its rings snaking from chimneys, from emptying factories,
from their bitten lips.
Unlike writers, they have no reason to distrust their hands.
They did not ask for what they hold.
They will not mourn as they are told.

Imperatives

Avoid the headlines. Analogise your pain. Remember that the crisis is nothing like the last one which was nothing like the one before that or the one before that. Honour the specifics. Honour only your sleeping schedule. Change the subject. Change your clothes. Check your emails. Check your balance. Sharpen your rage. Boycott sugar. Stretch. Stop eulogising the elders and actually call them for once. Downward dog. Rearrange the wide rooms of your orchestrated futures. Abandon the religion of task management. Like always, it will be easier to harm those closest to you. Try to be more imaginative with your cruelty. Better yet, share your grief. There's more than enough to go around. Don't replace sheep with the arithmetic of ambulance sirens. Like any poet worth their salt, think about the moon. Don't write about it, though. This is not a time for poems which is exactly why it is a time for poems. Lose track of your inadequacies. Pass hours and blame under the table. Broadcast your apologies. Leave a blood-red handprint on your front door. Paint your nails with what's left. Sign the petition. Send the form. Befriend yourself. Learn the undertones of your favourite body lotion. Study the shape of a faded scar. This, like the chipped mug, is your territory. Make a playlist for no one in particular. Live open-mouthed and open-ended. Invent new and increasingly desperate ways to use your hands. Clap. Cry. Light a rag. Renounce.

YOMI ṢODE

Yomi Ṣode is an award-winning Nigerian-British writer. His debut collection *Manorism*, published by Penguin in 2022 alongside a stage adaptation at London's Southbank Centre, was shortlisted for the Rathbones Folio Prize 2023 and the T.S. Eliot Prize 2022. He was shortlisted for the Brunel International African Poetry Prize 2021, and received the Jerwood Compton Poetry Fellowship in 2019. Yomi's acclaimed one-man show *COAT* toured nationally to sold-out audiences, including at the Brighton Festival, Roundhouse Camden and the Battersea Arts Centre. In 2020 his libretto *Remnants*, written in collaboration with award-winning composer James B. Wilson and performed with Chineke! Orchestra, premièred on BBC Radio 3. In 2021, his play, *and breathe...* premièred at the Almeida Theatre to rave reviews. Yomi is a member of Malika's Poetry Kitchen. He is the founder of BoxedIn, First Five, The Daddy Diaries, and mentorship programme, 12 in 12.

The Exhibition 2.0

Tiziano Vecelli, known as Titian
Portrait of Laura dei Dianti
1520–1525
Oil on canvas

The African page, more an ornament than a human being. His jacket of contrasting yellows, greens and oranges. His eyes look up towards his *mistress* – and beneath his wary gaze, I wonder whether he questions the whereabouts of his parents. The mistress wears a blue satin dress, with a gold sash wrapped around her chest. Her hand rests gently on the page's shoulder. The darker the ornament's hue, the greater the perception of the sitter's wealth – the greater the suggestion of his inferiority. Wearing clothes he did not choose, feigning a love I'm not sure he feels, he is a status symbol not required to speak or think for himself. None of this could have been given freely: this is how he was immortalised in an image, long enough for us to encounter him.

Artist unknown	Orazio Mochi
Jacques Francis	African Court Jester
1548	1600–1610
Human life glimpsed in court records	Sculpture in bronze

Jacques Francis, called an *uncivilised man* and a *slave*, though he is a freedman. Did Jacques think the times he dived to depths deeper than his white counterparts, risking his life to retrieve goods benefitting an empire, would change the way this culture saw him? Did he think he was one of them and not a lab rat consigned to the unknown ocean? Am I not Jacques Francis, being told my writing is not poetry? Though I craft each stanza hoping to be accepted. Am I not the *African Court Jester*? Bound to the curiosity and dangers of my body, bound to the outcome should I cease to entertain. We do not often speak this thought. There is no room for the jester to say *Enough*, unlike Jacques, soon clocking that educated verbal performances are not what is desired of slaves. To speak requires thinking, to think means feeling, and to feel means Jacques, the jester – me – are of flesh and bone, like them.

We are nothing like them.

Franco Rosso (dir.)
Beefy and Blue's Rage
1980
5 minutes 37 seconds
Excerpts from *Babylon*

'Don't talk fucking Black!'

The morning Beefy's rage finally finds speech, Ronnie is laid out on the floor, one hand to his bleeding nose. Earlier, Beefy shouted, *This is my country, lady*, and I felt him. *And it's never been fucking lovely*. His rage was speaking for the African page, for Jacques, for the jester. It's always been a fucking tip – he was speaking for me – for as long as I can remember! He was speaking for his friend, Blue, whose rage reached a boiling point, and tipped, till he stabbed one of them. A reaction to the violence of sus laws, poverty, unemployment and nationalists. His body, like Beefy's, had absorbed too much over time. All the outburst of an uprising, all the warrior charge of a song: *Nah nah nah nah nah nah, we cyan tek no more ah dat!* All these Black men a stage, an exhibition – until the spotlight turns back on their oppressors.

12:05 in North London, Thinking about Kingsley Smith

My Mother made me wear steel-plated boots for my first day in school. She painted Black on each boot. Black on Black like a blessing. With pride, she enrolled the name, Yomi. Something unfamiliar to my tongue. *She never heard African bubu scratcher or you AF's.* My Mother never heard the mocking.

Bullies also wore suits. Though she never heard their *You won't amount to anything,* chatter, she beat me bad, beat me scared, beat me sorry. She beat me for being rude to the teachers. How dare I speak of wrongdoing, when they have my best interest at heart.

My Mother worked twice as hard in England. Her profession in Nigeria meant little on the paper it's written on here. She now cares for elderly white people, who in the past refused the help of a Black woman, then purposely shat on the floor for her to wipe. She would call me most Christmas nights from work, seeing if I was ok. Maybe, as comfort for herself. Also, the thought that one day, this will all be worth it.

My Mother, now a Grandmother, has yet to be offered a suit. She wonders, why? Her kindness. Did it ever mean anything? She hears the language used towards her Grandson now. *What do they mean assessment, and disruptive?* ~~She yells~~. *Liars! Junior, you can try, try and try even more, but they will still look through you like you do not exist, or for you to bleed until they can even take you seriously!*

My mother, tells me to tell the bullies in suits, *Leave him alone!* Or she will come to the school to deal with each of them, one by one. Proudly, I watch my mother, slowly feeling the muscles in my face squeeze as it turns to a bittersweet stare.

An Ode to Bruv, Ting, Fam and, on Occasion, Cuz & My Man

for Kareem Parkins-Brown & Isaiah Hull

As in

a language, knotted through an ancestry.
Shapeshifting whenever in harm's reach.

Bruv, as in Brother, Bro,
Bredda, Bruh, or Bravvvvvvvv

                                                                As in

                                        Bruv! I passed dat ting!

                        Well done bruv. Can you believe dat ting aired my man?

                *Rah, so you just casually switch to a next ting, than celebrate
                                                        my ting fam?*

                        Nah bro, you know I'm just tryna be like youuu fam!

As in

how nameless yet known.
Dis ting, a warped reality
to my man, my man &
my man. A ting as sweet
as a Ting. Having breddas
scratch their heads, àwọn
ọdẹ.

How dextrous a language.
How my man & my man done
a madness. How one can build
castles in what that means.

How owned that we hear its hiss
on the wrong tongues, & rattling
of bones in its misspeak.

How, like air, it cannot be grabbed
by those who've pillaged enough.
Those that fed themselves full
of a people.

                                             As in
                              dis ting. A spiritual ting.
                        Aneephya! From the grave,
                                        to the youth

DEGNA STONE

Originally from the Midlands, Degna Stone is a poet and poetry editor based in north-east England. They are co-founder and former managing editor of *Butcher's Dog* poetry magazine, a contributing editor at *The Rialto*, and an associate artist with *The Poetry Exchange*. Magazine and online publications include: *The Black Light Engine Room, Diamond Twig, Ink, Sweat & Tears, The Ofi Press* and *The Rialto*. Appearances include: Durham Book Festival, Newcastle Poetry Festival, StAnza International Poetry Festival, Stoke Literary Festival, Leeds Lit Festival, Sunderland Literature Festival and BBC Radio 3's *The Verb*.

They received a major Northern Writers' Award for poetry in 2015, hold an MA in Creative Writing from Newcastle University, and are currently undertaking a PhD in Cultural Studies at Northumbria University. Their debut full-length poetry collection *Proof of Life on Earth* was published by Nine Arches Press in 2022.

Walltown Crags

lose your sense of god / walk out to devil's causeway and strike a deal / this place at the edge of an empire / is where you test the limit of your senses / tread ancient rights of way / under skies empty of heaven / fall into the footsteps of your ancestors / you are a part of this land / the weight of silence settles on your shoulders / this is the place where you remember who you are

Proof of Life on Earth

i.m. Marian Williams

In the museum of half a million objects
my eyes don't know where to settle,
so I lose myself amongst the maze of cases.

Every surface is covered, every cabinet
packed with artefacts, acquisition numbers
tattooed conspicuously in precise white paint.

The guide says much of the collection
relates to how to attract a loved one,
how to survive, how to deal with grief —

In my private state of deferred grief, amidst
the ordered chaos of the present in conversation
with the past, I am drawn to the weapons of war.

In the Upper Gallery the tools we use to harm
each other, objects whose sole function is to cause
injury or death, are displayed according to type.

I learn that *the sword was developed purely
for human combat*, and that in most cultures
women and swords are rarely found.

The evolution of guns mirrors the evolution
of man: trial and error and experimentation.
Each new generation more efficient, more lethal.

There is a broadsword too heavy to carry,
and a Walther PP, too dangerous to be placed
in the hands of a poet. Objects out of bounds.

Instead I study a single late medieval boot,
one hundred hobnails hammered into its sole,
and a brass aquamanile in the form of a horse.

We can look but not touch, so I slip
into a minor state of sensory deprivation,
sketch the boot's layers of old animal skin,

try to conjure the wearer, and connect
with a time when technology evolved slowly,
where history was recorded at a human pace.

I imagine the aquamanile filled with water,
imagine purifying my hands of the trauma
of passing through the stages of life,

rinsing away the fear that comes from awaiting
the death of a loved one, and an ever-deepening
belief in the absence of any gods.

over {prep., adv}

after A. Van Jordan

1. Above or beyond: She sang along to *Somewhere Over the Rainbow*, never imagining her own shoes could be ruby slippers, could carry her away. When she was a girl, her imagination always led to trouble. She soon learned that daydreamers were fools. Bit by bit she locked her dreams inside. **2. Throughout the duration of**: Over the years it became apparent that they couldn't stand the sight, the smell, the thought of each other. **3. On the opposite side of**: They could barely hold a civil conversation over the dinner table. **4. In consideration**: She goes over the list of things that piss her off about him every nights she brushes her teeth too hard. The way he talks down to her as if she's stupid, the way he hates her friends, the way he made her think she loved him, needed him and then grew distant. She spits blood into the sink. **5. In repetition**: She scrawled T.L.N.D. across her schoolbooks, carved it around the empty inkwell on her desk. Did she really believe back then that true love never dies? Love is not a constant. You must fall in love over and over and over again. **6. In reference to, concerning**: *What are we fighting over?* **7. Too great, excessive**: Her mother always told her she was oversensitive. 8. Through all parts of: She stands naked in front of the bathroom mirror looking over her body, running her hands over her skin, trying to remember what it felt like when he touched her. **9. Recovered from the effects of**: Though there was never an exact date, she marked every birthday that would have passed. *How can you celebrate the birthday of someone never born? Why aren't you over it by now?* **10. Submerge or bury**: She sank down and let the water close over her head.

JENNIFER LEE TSAI

Jennifer Lee Tsai is a poet, editor and critic. She was born in Bebington and grew up in Liverpool. She is a Ledbury Poetry Critic. Her poetry and criticism are widely published in magazines and journals including *Poetry London*, *The Poetry Review*, *The Telegraph*, *The TLS* and *The White Review*. Her debut poetry pamphlet is *Kismet* (ignitionpress, 2019). In 2019, she was awarded an AHRC scholarship to undertake doctoral research in Creative Writing at the University of Liverpool. She received a Northern Writers Award for Poetry in 2020. Her second poetry pamphlet *La Mystérique* (2022) was published by Guillemot Press. She is a winner of the 2022 Women Poets' Prize.

About Chinese Women

Suicide without a cause, or silent sacrifice for an apparent cause which, in our age, is usually political: a woman can carry off such things without tragedy, without even drama.

JULIA KRISTEVA

I

I return to a former self,
ghost or shadow self emerging from a glimmering light;

Woolf's 'luminous halo, a semi-transparent envelope surrounding us from the beginning of consciousness to the end'

Life as circularity,
                    inevitable return to a womb-like space,
                                        a space of the maternal?

Where do the dead go after they die? In what nether region do they inhabit?

Where did the Hakka people come from? Peripatetic tribe from north-east China.

She comes from people without a home, or fixed position. She is condemned and doomed to wander looking for her place in history.

I conjure up the past, delving into the recesses of unknown memory and time.

I am returning to the source. The original source. The point of all our origin. But these origins go further back beyond Western tradition, beyond the story of holy innocence fabricated in the myths of Adam and Eve, and the notion of a God the father. And it does not reside in the maternal womb either, that place of warmth and nurturance, which begins with love.

I invite mystery. I return to our innate energy, excavating deeply layer upon layer of our consciousness.

I breathe in the light; I inhale deeply and exhale...

Where is the point of our origin?

I am digging deep. I have to go further than the surface of things, back through space and time.

I uncover hidden treasure buried for centuries, and carefully retrieve it for future purposes.

Filtering through the coloured papers of memory, those delicate, fragile and carefully processed pieces of our past and history felt in my bones and body.

In the beginning there was the Word. And the Word is me. My words become me, and I become the word, a flurry of mixed phrases, half-spoken sentences, articulate in their gibberish.

I try to find the language that defines me, become a whirling dervish, caught up in a veil of spinning letters. They fly around me, and I try to catch them.

In the beginning there was the Word.

I am the signifier, the signified, signifying everything and nothing.

Once, I danced myself into a trance to find my grandmother's spirit.

When I felt it, my body shattered into tiny fragments.

Syncope – an absence of the self, time faltering, head spinning with a sudden vertigo.

Silent grandmother, guardian of secrets, please speak to me.

And when the repressed return to reclaim themselves, it will be terrifying.

II

A black and white family photograph taken in Hong Kong. The year is 1957 or 1958? My mother doesn't know exactly. There are three generations of *Hakka* people in the photograph – my grandparents and their children, my grandfather's brother and his family and my great-grandmother.

Hakka means guest families. They are nomadic migrants, renowned for their fortitude and resilience. In the nineteenth century, in clan wars against the Punti people, they built walled villages to protect themselves. My mother tells me how hard they worked all day in the fields growing rice, sweet potatoes, yams. There was no gas, no paraffin. They worked under the sun all day until it went dark. They sold their crops. The name of the area they lived in was called Kuk Po. It was inhabited by seven clans – Sung (宋), Lee (李), Ho (何), Tsang (曾), Cheng (鄭), Ng (吳) and Yeung (楊). Today, Kuk Po is an abandoned village, inhabited by many ghosts. The town borders the Frontier Closed Area…

Three women sit in the middle of the photograph. In the centre, the matriarch – my great grandmother sits. In front of her, she parades her favourite grandson, my uncle. On her mother's lap, my mother is a toddler, looking at the camera with bewildered eyes.

My grandfather, whom I hardly know, stands as a young, handsome man. My grandmother, gazes at the camera with seemingly sad eyes but she is difficult to read. Is she angry, troubled, distrustful, resentful? What is it that flickers beneath the surface, caught in this singular moment?

I can see my aunt's features in my grandmother, her big, round eyes, her wide nose and full lips. All the women are dressed in dark clothes, the men in white shirts, the children in a mixture of traditional dress and western clothes and what I find interesting about the photo is that the women are placed in the middle. No one is smiling; even the children look sombre. It's as though someone has died. And someone will die, in two or three years after this photograph is taken – my grandmother. She will take her own life and leave her children behind. An eternal mystery; unreadable cypher. From generation to generation, an irretrievable grief, an irrevocable loss reverberates.

My mother will become motherless at the age of three or four, she will inherit a wicked stepmother but earn the guilt-stricken love of her grandmother trying to make amends for her sins. My mother tells me how her grandmother really loved her and saved an apple only for her every day. No one else had an apple, only me.

Mirror, Mirror on the wall. Who is the fairest of us all?

Do you remember her, Mammy? What was she like?

Like you, I remember many things from childhood. I can still remember seeing her foaming at the mouth after she drank the weed killer. I think she mustn't have drunk very much because she could still walk home back to the village. They tried to ferry her across the harbour to the city, but it was too late. Of course, she died.

Her body lies somewhere in an unmarked grave on the beach in San Tao. No one knows where she is buried. In recent years, my aunt bought a shrine for her in a cemetery in Hong Kong.

The Yellow Woman

> We say Black women, brown women, white women, but not yellow women. Is it because this last category is no longer relevant? Or it because this outdated locution, rooted in nineteenth-century racial nomenclature, names something inadmissible, what is very much a mute but live animus today?
>
> ANNE ANLIN CHENG

Where is she?

Who is she?

She runs through the streets of England –

         a girl like you or me, except (s)he is not you or me.

Invisible or not seen
         in the Western imaginary.

A theoretical black hole, a residue of critical fatigue

She is mute or muted
she is absent
missing
silent or silenced.

An object or material?
The finest of silks,
a prized vase or dish from the Ming, Tang or Song dynasty,
pottery or ceramics behind the glass case of a museum.

Come see! Come see!
A thing of beauty is a joy forever!

Is the yellow woman injured – or is she injured enough?

Her ghost lingers in the shadows
Smile of a china doll.
Plum blossom trembles in the breeze
The quiver of a zither

Scream of a dragon lady
A geisha who serves tea
An ornamental butterfly –

See how she spreads her wings!
Then – watch her now soar and escape –

She has abandoned her body.
She is, temporarily, in a state of weakness.
The heart contracts.
It is numbed by fog, then vanishes.
She is no longer herself but remains more and more herself.

Consciousness expands –
freedom from the narrow borders of self.
She is a wave in the ocean
a ray in the sunlight
gravity with the stars
a raindrop, a moonbeam.

Who is she writing for?
A future version of herself.
Why?
Because she doesn't exist yet.
Is that not very narcissistic?
No.
Why?
Because she doesn't exist yet.
What do you mean?
She is not a person. She is not even human.
Her own mother told her that many years ago.
When she started a secret rebellion.

ROUND 2

MONA ARSHI

Mona Arshi is a poet, novelist and essayist. She initially trained as a human rights lawyer and worked at Liberty as a litigator before she started writing poetry in 2009, completing her Masters in poetry in 2011 at the University of East Anglia Her debut collection *Small Hands* (Pavilion) won the Forward Prize for Best First Collection in 2015.

Her poems, interviews and essays have been published in *The Times*, *The Guardian*, *Granta* and *The Times of India* as well as on the London Underground. She has collaborated with dancers ('Dancing Words'), musicians (Vidal Montgomery) and fashion (JIGSAW and Gallery Unconfined). She has read at various festivals as well as at the BFI, Southbank, British Museum, Mansion House and galleries throughout the UK. Mona has worked as a tutor for the Arvon Foundation as well as The Poetry School. She has judged the National Poetry Competition, the Foyle Schools Poetry Competition, the Forward Prize and the T.S. Eliot Prize and more recently the *Sunday Times* Young Writer of the Year Award.

Her second collection *Dear Big Gods* was published by Liverpool University Press's Pavilion Poetry imprint in 2019. In 2020 she was writer in Residence at Cley Marshes in Norfolk. Her essays have been published in *The Yale Review* and by PEN UK. In 2020 she was appointed Honorary Professor at the University of Liverpool and is a fellow in creative writing at Trinity College Cambridge until 2024. Her debut novel was published by And Other Stories in 2022 and was included in the Jhalak, Desmond Elliot, Republic of Consciousness and Goldsmith prize lists, and was also Book of the Week in *The Telegraph* (described there as 'a gorgeous novel in sensitivity') and *The Week Magazine*. Mona is an Ambassador for PEN International and a Fellow of the Royal Society of Literature.

Yellows

Last summer was the first time
I caught a glimpse of my soul.
A daughter had saved me from

drowning in a yellow-tiled pool.
On the water's surface a pair of nascent
antlers were melting away in the sunlight.

I am small, I am small, I say
shivering in my towel, bare and humble
in my child's arms, my eyes fixed poolside.

The second time was on a train,
the rapeseed stinging my eyes –
that blizzard of yellow –

she was resting in the corner of
the window, hitched on a bee,
dust-bathing in pollen. *Too soon-not yet*,

I whispered to the tiny thing
and coward that I am, flipped
them both out of the window.

Then on the longest day a boy was falling…
he fell into Richmond, this stowaway,
fell into Surrey and I saw the soul

of this boy, the structure, its plumage,
parachute out of the plane dressed
in all its paraphernalia.

Now I am more circumspect.
I rescue petals from tea-cups,
appease wasps at my table, praying

they've all repaired themselves fully in
the ancient ways, in their yellow frocks,
in those scented fields.

February

it's february and
snowing
like it's supposed to

I am searching
lifting paper
rifling through

the drawers I
have just
written *beauty*

is incidental
beauty is circumstantial
my hands find

a little box with
the milk teeth
their dozen

half-dissolved
roots attached
still

entrapped in plastic
my friend has
told me

she witnessed
curls of vapour
leave

the earthbody
of her father or
maybe

it was a shadow of
his soul
extending his

hand not knowing
its place
I am

thinking of
the last time
we met

when you told
me about the
green flash

on the horizon and
how close
can we get?

I won't
soften it
seeing the first

spectral elbow
was like
a blow

to the head
even in
swiftness of snow

each fleck
expecting
a reply
through the window

Arrivals

the dead
   how they arrive
in slow trailers

on buses
   the untidy dead
though they carry

no baggage
   they hold
unguarded photographs

and small words
   spoken in
suburban kitchens

or rare marbles
   the colour of citrine
never traded

in childhood
   some wait
by oaken shelters

they exercise such
   tender caution
shoelaces tied

the perfumed dead
   on that long road
the rain spitting from

a sideways direction
   why should there
not be rain

by and by
   and why shouldn't
birds still

stamp for worms
   whilst cats'-eyes blink
in the distance

from My Little Sequence of Ugliness

the departed as leaves

sometimes I
talk to leaves
where are your

flight muscles
I say
leaves

will you ignore
the flow
of auxin?

this is a world
heavy
with over

corrections
and then
there are the

leaves

from The Book of Hurts

I received a parcel
a box
it contained all

the old hurts
their legs
were flailing

like upturned
insects
in motion

I touched one
it was razor sharp
it became then

a naked apple
I held it up
to the light

by its stalk
it began to brown
it began to talk

JAY BERNARD

Jay Bernard, FRSL, FRSA, is a multidisciplinary writer and artist from London whose work is rooted in social histories. Jay was named *Sunday Times* Young Writer of the Year 2020 and winner of the 2017 Ted Hughes Award for their first collection *Surge*, a queer exploration of the archives surrounding the 1981 New Cross Fire. Recent work includes *Joint*, a poetic-play about the history of joint enterprise; *Crystals of this Social Substance*, a sound installation at the Serpentine pavilion in which eight young people explore the concept of money; *Complicity*, a pamphlet that explores the changing face of London via the Tate collection; and *You Are Invited Back to the Land*, a graphic intervention displayed in Tate Britain's 1980s gallery. Jay received a 2022-23 DAAD literature fellowship in Berlin and a 2023-24 fellowship at the Institute for Ideas and Imagination.

from **Surge**

Clearing

He takes my head and places it in a plastic bag

downstairs, two officers stamp their feet
blow into their hands

the windows are cups of water filled with winter

he holds the bag open, searching
for a gaze to meet

cold
thirsts at the bones

he doesn't see me standing there
he doesn't hear me speak

an officer circles the front yard leaning
back to see the smoke

                or is it steam

is it fire or water that can bring a child back

elide that which is heavy in his hand
and that which watches from the corner of the room

this house is a gas lamp
soot frosts its glasswhite gut

the officer closes his eyes
two blank pennies in a fount

from the bag I watch his face turn away
from the corner his body bending towards mine

the officer said – oh, it's very common for culprits to go missing – I said my son isn't a culprit, and how dare he imply it – and one of the officers stood up by the window and looked out – he didn't want to look us full in the eye – he made it clear, he made it clear – from the moment he set foot in the house – the moment he set foot – what he thought of us – and when they come back a few days later – I think the Tuesday, I think the Tuesday – they said what were you wearing on the night of the fire? – I said probably – probably – your new trousers – and he said was you wearing a yellow shirt? – I said yes – Brown shoes? – I said yes – and he took out the items from a plastic bag – he took your things from a plastic bag – and he says does this look like it? Does this look like it belongs to you? – I says yes – and he says do you recognise this key? – I said why don't we try it – and we struggled – and it fit – I'm sorry, I'm so sorry, I'm so sorry – so I said what are you sorry for? I want to see my son – stammer, stammer, they say they don't think it is a good idea – I said, I am your father – I said, I said, I am your father – your father – I want to see you –

        – they led us down to a room – and on the table there you was – no face, nothing to speak of – I said – I said – this is the body where you found the clothes? – nod, nod – So I said, it must be you – this must be my son

                                    -

You came, dad –

        – I had been lying there all night – and I couldn't move. I opened my eyes and I was in the house and everything was black, dad – I had been at the party a few hours and I didn't know any-thing about what happened, dad – and I felt someone touch me, but I was stiff, dad – I never been so stiff before – I tried to say it's me, it's me – but they were looking

at me so strangely, dad – like he couldn't stand to look at me –
couldn't stand the sight of me – Police always looked at me like
that – and he turned me over – and he took the shirt from
under me, and they wrapped me in a blanket and drove me
here – and I was lying there waiting for you, dad – across the
table, there were bodies, dad – Twisted, dad – no heads – like
screaming branches of a tree, dad – loads of them, loads of
them, I swear – and I heard them say – they were saying –

And then you came and I was calling out to you, dad
– and I know you heard me because here we are, dad – come
back – don't bury me – I can't stand it – I can barely stand it
when the lights go off – and I'm here – and spend the whole
night listening for you dad – I want to crawl between mum and
you – in your bed, in your sheets, dad – that's the only kind of
burying I want –

KAYO CHINGONYI

Kayo Chingonyi, FRSL, was born in Zambia in 1987, and moved to the UK at the age of six. He is a fellow of the Civitella Ranieri Foundation. In 2012 he was awarded a Geoffrey Dearmer Prize by The Poetry Society and was Associate Poet at the Institute of Contemporary Arts (ICA) in 2015. His first full-length collection, *Kumukanda*, won the Dylan Thomas Prize and a Somerset Maugham Award. Kayo was a Burgess Fellow at the Centre for New Writing, University of Manchester before joining Durham University as Assistant Professor of Creative Writing. He is a writer and presenter for the music and culture podcast *Decode* on Spotify, and poetry editor at Bloomsbury. His most recent collection, *A Blood Condition*, was shortlisted for the Forward Prize for Best Collection, the T.S. Eliot Prize and the Costa Poetry Award. He was elected a fellow of the Royal Society of Literature in 2022.

Kumukanda

Since I haven't danced among my fellow initiates,
following a looped procession from woods at the edge
of a village, Tata's people would think me unfinished –
a child who never sloughed off the childish estate
to cross the river boys of our tribe must cross
in order to die and come back grown.

I was raised in a strange land, by small increments:
when I bathed my mother the days she was too weak,
when auntie broke the news and I chose a yellow suit
and white shoes to dress my mother's body,
at the grave-side when the man I almost grew to call
dad, though we both needed a hug, shook my hand.

If my alternate self, who never left, could see me
what would he make of these literary pretensions,
this need to speak with a tongue that isn't mine?
Would he be strange to me as I to him, frowning
as he greets me in the language of my father
and my father's father and my father's father's father?

The Colour of James Brown's Scream

for Steve McCarthy and Todd Bracey

I have known you by many names
but today you are Larry Levan,
your hand on the platter in the smoky
room of a *Garage* regular's memory.
You are keeping 'When Doves Cry'
in time, as you swing your hips,
and sweat drips from your hair
the colour of James Brown's scream.

King of King Street, we are still moving
to the same sound, though some
of us don't know it is your grave
we dance on, cutting shapes
machismo lost to the beat –
every road man is a sweetboy
if the DJ plays 'Heartbroken'
at just the right time for these jaded feet.
Teach us to shape-shift, Legba,
you must know I'd know your customary
shuffle, that phantom limp, anywhere;
that I see your hand in the abandon
of a couple, middle of the floor,
sliding quick and slick as a skin-fade
by the hand of a Puerto Rican clipper-man
who wields a cutthroat like a paintbrush.
Let us become like them, an ode
to night, ordering beer in a corporeal
language from a barman who replies
by sweeping his arms in an arc,
Willi Ninja style, to fix a drink our lips
will yearn for, a taste we've been
trying to recreate ever since.

Nyaminyami: 'water can crash and water can flow'

who gave them   licence   to live   here
who brought them   succour refuge
what gave them   the right
to come between   this centuries-old   love
what do they know   of love
who have not loved   outside   human time
this wall they built   in all their wisdom
can only delay   our union
those   who know water   know

eventually water will pass through
even   the smallest gap   in what appears
to the human eye   to be   a solid mass

Nyaminyami: epilogue

it is said that after the concrete
after the rain
after the valley
shifted from its old ways
all that remained
of nyaminyami
was a small statue
marking the place

a fish-headed snake
a caption
consigning the river god
to fable
as if all this water
flowed here by some accident
as if the old ways
were only stories

but to this day pilgrims
sometimes see a momentary swell
in the course of the river
and those who recognise these eddies
know this to be nyaminyami testing
the limits of human ingenuity
calling out to a lover who is constant
as the motion of water

RISHI DASTIDAR

Rishi Dastidar's poetry has been published by the *Financial Times*, *New Scientist*, and the BBC amongst many others. He is a consulting editor at *The Rialto* magazine. A poem from his debut *Ticker-tape* (Nine Arches Press) was included in *The Forward Book of Poetry 2018*. A pamphlet, *the break of a wave*, was published by Offord Road Books in 2019, and a second book, *Saffron Jack* (Nine Arches Press), was published in 2020. He is editor of *The Craft: A Guide to Making Poetry Happen in the 21st Century* (Nine Arches Press), and also co-editor of *Too Young, Too Loud, Too Different: Poems from Malika's Poetry Kitchen* (Corsair). His third collection, *Neptune's Projects*, was published by Nine Arches Press in 2023. He also reviews poetry for *The Guardian* and is a trustee of *Wasafiri*.

The Brexit Book of the Dead

Because that's what this is,
that's what we're writing
within this geopolitical Bardo
where we – sorry, a decisive

majority of us – has decided
that nostalgia is the best form
of statecraft to respond to a
future of heatproof algorithms

fighting wars that the humans
don't survive. I believed it
once too, that currency unions
decay but nations never die,

that subsidiarity was a theory
never tested, that the *acquis*
was common the way silk
handcuffs are. But then war

never killed our glory, and we
were never de-illusioned, just
disillusioned – why can't we
play the Blitz every week please?

So now we wait outside this
Berlaymont purgatorio,
dreaming of lions swimming
across la Manche, unicorns

conquering continents, the people's
bloodhounds chasing complexity's
fox. Look! we have Dover's
liberating cliff edge coming up,

because we are never freer
than when we are falling to
victory over the imperial lorry
park formerly known as Kent –

and is that RMS *Dambusters* we
see gunning towards the fishing
fields? To bellow and buccaneer
hotly is the only way to die chums!

In the next place, the cherries
are there to be picked, and the
sound of Lord North squealing,
'Lads, someone's fucked up

more than me!' is sweet nectar
to Empire 2.0, and we forget
that the answer to the question is:
the dead are perfectly sovereign.

Time takes a moment

There's snow on my daffodils this morning,
and time takes a moment to wonder
what it has done in springing spring early,
pretending it is single-minded, endless flow

when it is actually eddies, reverses, stops,
starts, sudden lurches, minutes of intense
focus. Then it says: You should be looking
so hard apertures break, trying to pin

this random arrangement of light down
to mourning tracking pixels, capture this now
because all your nows make up you

and who would you rather be? A flower
waking up cold is as beautiful as you;
it's worth being still to remember that.

Neptune's concrete crash helmet

I rest my head for a moment on the cool concrete wall
of the art gallery and in its undulations I can feel the past
trying to break out of its unexpected vertical tomb.

I could rub the back of my head into one of the grooves,
wear it away, erode it imperceptibly over a day's aeon
until I could place my head right back into the crevasse,

a temporary sarcophagus, an extra heavy-duty crash helmet.
This of course might be an over-reaction to the images
I've just seen: a world melting, gangsters wearing dresses

and razor'd scars of silver stars, lakes of petrol waiting
for paper boats to be sailed upon them, as if Neptune had
said yes to a sponsorship deal from [insert oil company name

here] but only lately realised that the proposed replacement
for a rapidly drying Aral Sea might not have been everything
promised in the brochure. Caveat emptor, as we all should have

said in 1764 when Hargreaves spun Jenny, but how could any
of us know that coal + steam would equal not just movement
but the end? I might stay in here, it keeps my head cool.

EDWARD DOEGAR

Edward Doegar is a writer, poet and editor based in London. He is a consulting editor at *The Rialto* and was the commissioning editor of the Poetry Translation Centre between 2018 and 2021. His pamphlet *For Now* was published by clinic in 2017 and a text written in collaboration with the artist Shakeeb Abu Hamdan was published by Kelder Press in 2022. His latest work, *sonnets*, will be published by Broken Sleep Books in 2023.

from **The English Lyric**

The rain is English rain –
Rain I have known all my life –
It falls medieval, new,

And neither. Nor do I
Claim to belong to the tribe.
And yet these words, this rain.

from **The English Lyric**

Dusk is its own tense, 'no longer'
    Returning to 'again'. Mud
Thickens the pace; the mossed gate,
    Sodden hollow, bars a right

Of way, ineffectual but adamant.
    A crow articulates the near-
Dark; it is large and close. Fear
    Breeds familiar words. England –

Described by its small possessions,
    Its grown boundaries – consoles
Wrongly. The hedgerow, a natural
    Order, ticks with justified

Theory, so the distance necessary,
    To observe all against all
As brute harmony, is of light
    Made. Thus, tradition maintains

The premise induced upon
   Us only for our reason to
'Prevail' (against all sense). Nearly
   Gone, the fields have given

Their every definition to the sky.
   It is almost clear; anyone
Might read their destiny there,
   Plotting a line through dots.

After After Remainder

for Sarah Macdonald

what I hadn't expected was	what I hadn't remembered
the exact variety of yellow	that was these several yellows
the inside-yuck of custard	and the air-digested quality
of the skin	that jaundiced view of things
that turns a cliché true	off-putting as the perfect yoke
of any rhymed word	heard only for its own sake
as the chain of metaphor	insists on the concept of slavery
another victimless crime	of the untethered mind
which is a view I contemplate	but can't confront
as if the stairs led somewhere	to a pattern on the wall
as if the pattern on the wall	recalled the details
in a book I haven't read	but can quote and forget

INUA ELLAMS

Born in Nigeria, Inua Ellams is a poet, playwright and performer, graphic artist and designer. He facilitates workshops in creative writing where he explores recurring themes in his work – identity, displacement and destiny – in accessible, enjoyable ways for participants of all ages and backgrounds.

His awards include: Edinburgh Fringe First Award 2009, the Liberty Human Rights Award, Live Canon International Poetry Prize, Kent & Sussex Open Poetry Competition, *Magma* Poetry Competition, Winchester Poetry Prize, a Black British Theatre Award and the Hay Festival Medal for Poetry.

He has been commissioned to produce work by the Royal Shakespeare Company, National Theatre, Tate Modern, Louis Vuitton and by BBC Radio and Television. His poetry books include *Candy Coated Unicorn and Converse All Stars* (flipped eye), *The Wire-Headed Heathen* (Akashic Books), *The Half God of Rainfall* (Fourth Estate) and *The Actual* (Penned in the Margins). His plays include *Black T-shirt Collection*, *The 14th Tale*, *Barber Shop Chronicles* and *Three Sisters*, published by Oberon.

As a curator, he founded: The Midnight Run (an arts-filled, night-time, urban walking experience); The Rhythm and Poetry Party (The R.A.P. Party), which celebrates poetry and music; Poetry + Film / Hack (P+F/H), which celebrates poetry and film; Redacted, which celebrates blackout poetry and conversation; and Anonyms, which explores naming and personal mythology. Inua also founded 05Fest, a festival putting poetry and words centre stage, uniting his live events and theatric works.

from **The Half God of Rainfall**

Ôrúnmilà, the God of vision and fiction,
whose unique knowing is borderless, whose wisdom
unmatched, who witnessed the light of all creation,

to whom all stories are lines etched deep in his palms,
from the heavens above Nigeria read the qualm
of oncoming conflict, shook his head and looked down.

– x –

The local boys had chosen grounds not too far from
the river, so a cooled breeze could blow them twisting
in the heat. The boys had picked clean its battered palms,

leaves left from previous years, to make this their grounding,
their patch, their pitch. These local lads levelled it flat,
stood two shortened telephone poles up, centring

both ends of the field. Then they mounted tyres, strapped
one atop each pole and stitched strips of fishing nets
to these black rims. Court lines were drawn in charcoal mashed

into a paste and the soil held the dark pigment,
the free throw lines' glistening geometry perfect.
They called it Battle Field, The Court of Kings, The Test,

for this was where warriors were primed from the rest,
where generals were honoured and mere soldiers crushed.
Basketball was more than sport, the boys were obsessed.

They played with a righteous thirst. There were parries, thrusts,
shields and shots, strategies and tactics, land won and
lost, duels fought, ball like a missile, targets | + | locked, such

97

that Ôgûn, the Ôrisà God of War, would stand
and watch. He'd stand and watch. The Gods were watching on.
One child, named Demi, was kept from play. He was banned.

He'd crouch on the edge of the court watching boys turn
and glide in the reach towards the rim, a chasm,
a cavernous emptiness between him and them.

He was banned from games for if they lost, tears would come.
Demi would drench his shirt, soak his classroom and flood
whole schools as once he'd done their pitch, the soil swollen,

poles sunk, it all turned to swamp for weeks. Their lifeblood,
the balletic within them, their game had been stalled.
They never forgave him turning their world to mud.

They resented more than they feared Demi and called
him 'Town Crier', loud, mercilessly chanting this
as they crossed over the brown orb, dribbling, they'd call

Town Crier! Watch this! They worshipped Michael Jordan, ripped
his moves from old games. They'd practise trash-talking, those
dark boys, skin singing to the heat. They'd try to fit

Nigerian tongues round American accents – close
but not close enough – *Dat all you ghot mehn? Ghottu
du betta mehn, youh mama so fat, giant clothes*

no fit cover her hass! till a fist-fight broke through
their game and war spilled out, the Gods laughing, the ball
r o l l i n g towards Demi…who, that day, bent to scoop

it up, desperate to join their lush quarrel and all
he asked for was one shot, the five foot four of him
quivering on the court. *No* said Bolu, stood tall,

the King of the court *You'll miss and cry. Boys, grab him!*
Demi fought in their grip, eyes starting to water,
Just one shot or I'll cry and drown this pitch he screamed,

his voice slicing the sky, clouds gathering over.
You small boy! You no get shame? Remember this belt?
Pass the ball before I whip you even harder!

But the King's voice hushed as the earth began to melt,
the soil dampen, telephone poles tilt and great tears
pool in Demi's wild eyes. Far off, Modúpẹ́ felt

that earth wane. Modúpẹ́, Demi's mother, her fears
honed by her child, knowing what danger wild water
could do let loose on land, left everything – her ears

seeking Demi's distinct sobbing – the market where
she worked, utter chaos in her wake, in her vaults
over tables stacked with fruits and fried goods, the air

       parting   for her, the men unable to find fault
in the thick-limbed smooth movement that was her full form.
Back at the court, Demi held on as the boys waltzed

around his pinned-down form beneath the threatening storm
One shot oh! Just one! the arena turning mulch
beneath them. Alarmed, the King yelled *Fine! But shoot from*

where you lay. Demi spat the soil out his mouth, hunched
till he could see one dark rim, gathered his sob back
into him and let fly the ball, his face down, crunched.

Years later Bolu would recount that shot. Its arch.
Its definite flight path, the slow rise, peak and wane
of its fall through the fishing net. Swish. Its wet thwack

on damp earth, the skies clearing, then silence. *Again*
Bolu said, pushing the ball to his chest. *Again.*
Demi, do it again. And the crowds went insane.

The rabble grew and swirled around them on the plain
of damp soil chanting *Again!* each time Demi drained
the ball down the net. Modúpẹ́ arrived and craned

her neck but couldn't glimpse Demi, so, a fountain
of worry, she splashed at one. *What happened? Tell me!*
You didn't see? Town Crier can't miss! He just became

the Rainman! Make it rain, baby! Yes! Shoot that three!
Ten more shots, each flawless, and they hoisted Demi
onto their shoulders, his face a map of pure glee.

Two things Modúpẹ́ would never forget – that glee
when Demi became the Rainman was the second.
The first, the much darker: how Demi was conceived.

SARAH HOWE

Sarah Howe is a British poet, academic and editor. Her first book, *Loop of Jade* (Chatto & Windus, 2015), won the T.S. Eliot Prize and the *Sunday Times*/PFD Young Writer of the Year Award, and was shortlisted for the Forward Prize for Best First Collection. Born in Hong Kong to an English father and Chinese mother, she moved to England as a child. She received an Eric Gregory Award from the Society of Authors for the work in her pamphlet, *A Certain Chinese Encyclopedia* (tall-lighthouse, 2009). She has performed her work at festivals internationally and on BBC Radio 3 and 4. Previous honours include a Hawthornden Fellowship and the Harper-Wood Studentship for English Poetry, as well as fellowships from Harvard University's Radcliffe Institute and the Civitella Ranieri Foundation. She is a Lecturer in Poetry at King's College London.

Sometimes I think

of the conkers I gathered once
　　　　　　　　when small myself
shucked of their green armour
　　　　　　　　and placed in
the glass bowl with the silvered
　　　　　　　　rim to admire
their mahogany sheen. Why am I
　　　　　　　　driving the train
off the rails? Two nights ago
　　　　　　　　my son woke
at four in the morning, crying
　　　　　　　　for me in the dark.
I placed my cool hand on his
　　　　　　　　forehead, licked
with winter clamminess. He said,
　　　　　　　　I had a bad
dream, softly, eyes tight shut, like
　　　　　　　　something heard
in a story. To my knowledge
　　　　　　　　his first – a concept
I'd thought he hadn't yet met
　　　　　　　　in his slender frame
of human experience. The CD
　　　　　　　　spinning leisurely
in the neighbour's ruined magnolia
　　　　　　　　glints its
ambit of tapering sun. As I kissed
　　　　　　　　his hair I had
a vision of his little head as a nut
　　　　　　　　or hollow shell.
A day or so later the conkers
　　　　　　　　issued a plague
of white wriggling worms from their seemingly
　　　　　　　　impermeable
glossy surfaces. Next morning over rice pops
　　　　　　　　I asked him

what he had dreamed. I listened like
                                        a mother
in a story, like listening could make it
                                        right.

Relativity

for Stephen Hawking

When we wake up brushed by panic in the dark
our pupils grope for the shape of things we know.

Photons loosed from slits like greyhounds at the track
reveal light's doubleness in their cast shadows

that stripe a dimmed lab's wall – particles no more –
and with a wave bid all certainties goodbye.

For what's sure in a universe that dopplers
away like a siren's midnight cry? They say

a flash seen from on and off a hurtling train
will explain why time dilates like a perfect

afternoon; predicts black holes where parallel lines
will meet, whose stark horizon even starlight,

bent in its tracks, can't resist. If we can think
this far, might not our eyes adjust to the dark?

from In the Chinese Ceramics Gallery

Earthenware model of a horse, unglazed

I, too, am a survivor.
My eroded coat dappled with lichen and stars.
My spirited tail has long
snapped off.

One millennium and then another
has wheeled on by
since the potter squatting on his dusty stool
thumbed my jowls

to the perfect roundness – a gesture
tender despite his production line – and nicked
my nostrils in this haughty flare. 'Stocky'
they called me

in the catalogue. I admit,
though hollow, my belly's a swollen gourd, buddha-full.
Ears pricked, mane brush-stiff,
my grin is quizzical, sometimes

even a grimace
behind the smudgy glass.
My hooves were long
buffed by clay ranks of imperial grooms.

Reserved for only the finest tombs
my kind maps out the trade
between civilisations –
one squat stallion for fifty bales of silk.

They rolled out the Silk Road before us
all the way to the walled city of Chang'an. The Han
emperor sent for us to fill
his echoing stables. He called us his *Tianma*,

'celestial horses', expecting our hardy stock
when the time came
at last to carry him up the narrow passes
into heaven. Some nights

I dream
of galloping across scrubby plains, the herd's sweat
tart as highland apricots around me –
far blue peaks retreating into memory.

Finely potted white glazed porcelain cup, Dehua ware

The English will forget who invented tea.
The way you might not guess, at first,
who made me, or why. The riddle of my origins

begins on a spinning wheel in Fujian, and ends
across two continents, with a silversmith
in Restoration London. I was made once

in a kiln's stark flame, feeling the translucent
glaze harden at my lip. Once cool, I was ready
for the kiss of alcohol. On summer evenings

between friends I brimmed with rice wine
no less refined than my own pure moon –
this white the Chinese call *Dehua*, but you

might know as *blanc-de-Chine*. Some twists
in my provenance are lost even to me:
a Pope's embassy, the halls of Versailles,

hands that held me up to the light in awe
at my lustre; placed me in locked cabinets
with seahorses, sextants, unicorns' tails.

But somewhere along the way that clod
of a smith insisted on gilding the lily.
I still remember the grip of those red-hot

scallops clamped around my rim, the strange
weight of this metal foot: never again
will I rise for a toast, bright against the night's

black silk. Remade in your imagination:
a sugar bowl. The brittle lumps would clink
against my delicately tapering sides

like coal into a pail. A creature of two
worlds, but belonging to none. Tell me,
is there a word for it in this new tongue?

Thinly potted porcelain Kraak dish painted in underglaze blue

Is there a word   for it in this new tongue?
The class of ships the Portuguese   named caravela,
and the French *caraque.*   Swift three- or four-masters,
they were *kraak*   to the Dutch, whose guttural pitch
I first heard from the sailors   who loaded us up
in our straw-stuffed crates: *Porcelain   vessels of diverse sorts*
the manifest called us   stowed by the hundreds
of thousands. Wares   named for those stately ocean-
going craft   sailing homeward from the mythic East
freighted with silk and damask   barrels of oakum
quicksilver, cinnabar, camphor.   Till disaster struck:
wrecked   off Goa's golden coast. As the cold current
of decades flowed past us, my stacked brethren   crusted
with barnacles   and powdery salt, mouths filling up with
silt. Still, some of us continued to gleam   like the shells
that yawned in those depths.   Dredged up from the dark
they pieced my fragments   back to wholeness, masked
each crack   with filler and skill. At last I came to rest
in this museum: a heavy Victorian vitrine, whose subtly
distorting glass recalled for me light   filtering through
underwater weeds. That night   in the Blitz was my last
near escape. Nothing like the kiln's   clarifying flames
that fire was   something else: ranks of precious artefacts
blasted into tinder, their cases   smashed; rare specimens
reduced to scattered feathers, shards   of wired bone.

In the aquarium, fish boiled   in their tanks or swilled
down drains; the model fishing boats   went up in smoke.
I've seen what it takes   to cradle a wreck back to the light.
Leaving the fractures for all to see   they rebuilt this place.
From the other side of ruin   we found safe passage.

ADAM LOWE

Adam Lowe (he/his, mostly) is a Leeds-born writer, performer and publisher who lives in Manchester. He is the UK's LGBT+ History Month Poet Laureate and was Yorkshire's Poet for 2012. He writes poetry, plays and fiction, and occasionally performs in drag as Beyonce Holes. Adam is a graduate of The Complete Works II and Obsidian, and had previously been mentored by Peepal Tree's Inscribe programme.

Adam is currently Chair of Black Gold Arts and sits on the board of Schools OUT UK, which founded LGBT+ History Month in the UK. He was one of the founders of #MEAction UK and also founded Young Enigma and *Vada Magazine*. Adam also runs Dog Horn Publishing.

Adam graduated with a BA and MA from the University of Leeds, and is studying for a PhD at the University of Manchester. His debut collection of poems *Patterflash* hits the shelves in June 2023.

Gingerella's Date

Girl, I only agreed because I was starvin' and sick
      of plain pasta. Not even tomatah!
I wo' dead skint, so I suggested we go fer a curry in Wigan.
      I thought it would scare'im off.

I hoped I'd have bad breath to keep him away. But anyway,
      he wo'n't havin' it.
He wanted me. So I played along. Ordered mixed starter
      with giant fuck-off king prawns,

lamb chops, samosas, the lot. Then I 'ad a butter chicken masala,
      and yer know I'm lactose intolerant!
Had that with garlic naan an' some pilau an' all. Then washed it
      down with a jug of mango lassi

and a bottle of rosé. I told the most filthy and obnoxious jokes.
      He lapped it up, didn't he!
Dirty ol' git woulda gone wi' me whatever I said. So I thought,
      fuck it! In for a penny, in for a pound!

I wo' outrageous, Bey! I ordered some kulfi ice cream too.
      Me gut wo' proper churning.
It wo' like a washing machine full of shit,
      you know what I mean?

Proper agony, right, but girl, it wo' proper good grub!
      I'd do it again right now if yer offered it me.
You know the curries where they just have that dirty grease
      in little puddles on the top?

Fuckin' fit, I tell yer! I ate the piggin' lot. And to top it all off,
      I had an Americano, just to make sure
I tasted proper rank. Then when the bill came, he looked
      so pleased. Slapped down twenny pound notes

like he wo' the Big I Am, right. But I could see what 'e wo' plannin'
        to do to my lily white ass,
and I tell yer now, Tanya Turner might be a slapper, but I
        ain't desperate, girl!

So I asked him to go get me some fags from the shop over't road
        before we left. Said I needed the loo, like,
you know. But when the man came to collect the money,
        I asked him for a doggy-bag

and told him to be quick. They got me all them leftovers
        wrapped up in less than two minutes.
I swear, they're proper geniuses down at Akbar's. And then,
        before 'e got back, I legged it, bags in 'and.

Only, he saw me, didn't he? Yelled after me like,
        'Oi! Where you fink you're off to?'
So I just waved him a pair of Vs and kept runnin'.
        I'll tell you what, though:

I need to stop smokin'. It fuckin' killed me runnin' up that hill.
        But it wo' worth it for that curry.
Worth it not to have to have plain spaghetti yet again.
        As I always say, *A girl's gotta eat!*

Elegy for the Latter-day Teen Wilderness Years

Joan, Trashley and Gingerella lived in a one-bed flat.
You'd never seen gurrls with more poise.

Our style made them sick. We had a cribbed language
others didn't understand and that gave us power.

We made the streetlights our spots. We were fierce, En Vogue.
We spoke in the high tones of grand dames, sashayed

and preened. There we were royalty. You should've seen
that long coat drag along the floor. We found fake fur in a skip

but wore it like mink. We were kings anyway. We made our lives
like that, rooting in bins round the back of Queens Court

living thrifty and spare. We would hold hands
and link arms on the march to some nearby-far after party.

We could leap across the horizon in electric blue heels
and banish bigots with a look. In dim chillouts, we made

community with chatter and gossip, hugs that bookended
us on the couch and on the bed. Ours was a private world

where our love for each other went unsaid and we
expressed our bonds in nicknames and twisting hips.

I was Beyoncé, you were Mariah, she was Violette.
We lived in the witching, hybrid hours, where the dark

and dim had pride of place. We were bold and wild, our songs
ricocheted against the naked heavens. Then the clouds

would thicken like stones. The morning would pour over us
like molten gold swallowing the glitter and bruises of night.

Reynardine for Red

You were Reynard, Fox King, red with cunning. I was on your tail.
I thought I was the hunter, but you led me deeper through
haunted woods. Though roots rose in treachery and thorns lay
snags along the path I made quick, eager to find the crux

of this wooded place. When the tangled boughs grew ragged
and the forest yawned, there I found your palace. It stood mighty,
yellow stone, all battlements and iron doors. You had a special knock
to get us inside. You showed me how to do it, as if I could still trust you,

even after you waylaid me. When the doors opened, I smelled
musk and filth, but your charm was enough to ignore it.
Inside, was like your love: labyrinthine, gnarly.
The dead ends were cauterised nerves.

I grew vexed, more obsessed, a vixen bride.
The mirrors were twisted, threw up cracked reflections
of my form. I spun around myself.
Reynard, your jaw is a gleaming knife in pink maw.

You paw shirt buttons to expose my heart. You took all that
you wanted. You sank fangs into skin, lapped at the muscle. You pulled
my fingernails from their beds. You threw me, hard, broke my bones,
my left eye corkscrewed from my face. You savaged

my nose, left it torn and bleeding. You smashed my fingers.
Grabbed by my hair, you pounded me into cruel stone.
You counted my teeth scattered on the floor. You tore my stomach
open, unravelled precious insides. This was how you preferred me.

But I refused to remain broken. I used spit and rheum
to glue my porcelain bones back together. I relied on rage to move
busted joints, to rise from the straw upon the cell floor. Every hair
on my skin bristled, every strand a flame. Red Dog-man, I was ready

to come for you. I scooped up my shattered teeth and wedged them
into gums. My smile, a wounded cherry. I reset the twisted arm,
leaned backwards to unbend my spine. I pressed on the wrenched nails,
till they settled like glass tombstones. I popped

the eye in place, its sickening kiss robbing me of appetite.
I bundled my guts back in, tucked tail between my legs. Rage turned
to design. I planned my lure. You liked weakness.
You loved me best when I begged and pleaded.

I hauled my tortured self through endless turns until I found your bedchamber
and lay before the door. When the loneliness took you, in the hours
between night and morning, you came out and found me. I blubbered,
and I mewled. I cried. You took me into your bed. Snuggled

against me for warmth. We fucked, and I tore a tuft
of red hair. You liked it. You yawned, slimed with cum, then slept.
Sneaky, nocturnal, I slid out of place and fashioned a rope of sheets.
Opened the window. I dropped to ground.

I ran through the forest, leaving the hair like a trail of breadcrumbs.
Come morning, while you still slept, I returned with hunters and their dogs.
The beasts sniffed your scent, tasted the essence of fur in air.
We arrived at the castle. The special knock let us in.

EILEEN PUN

Eileen Pun was born in New York, the daughter of Haitian and Haitian-Chinese parents. Partly based in Grasmere, England she also owns a farm in Abruzzo, Italy where she cultivates fruit, olives, exotic plants and is involved in several permaculture and art initiatives. More recently she has been collaborating with organic farms and artisans in Costa Rica in planting food forests, natural crafts and self-sufficiency. She has a bachelors degree in International Relations (University of Florida) and an MA in Creative Writing (Manchester Metropolitan University) where she won the 2009 Rosamond Prize for best collaboration in music and poetry. In 2010 her long poem/music theatre piece, *The Red Knot*, was performed by an orchestra from the Royal Northern College of Music and Central School of Speech and Drama, London and was featured on BBC Radio Manchester and Lancaster.

In 2011 Eileen was a Writers' Centre Norwich Escalator prizewinner and also awarded a writing and research grant by Arts Council England. In 2015 she received both a Northern Writers' Award and a Lisa Ullmann Travelling Scholarship (LUTSF) to China in support of her interdisciplinary work in movement and poetry. She is a fellow of the inaugural Sun Yat-Sen University International Writers' Residency, Guangzhou, where she presented her poetry and conducted a seminar for the English Poetry Studies Institute (EPSI). She also co-edited an edition of Xuezhi Hu's translation of Chuang Tzu as well as a book of Hu's Daoist writings.

In 2018 she was invited by Aboutime Dance Company, Lancashire, to create new performance work for Morecambe Bay Partnership, and wrote the sequence *Longways/Crosswise*. She also co-edited *Magma*'s 2018 Climate Change issue with Matt Howard and Fiona Moore. In 2019 she was awarded a bursary for Italian translators to the British Centre for Literary Translation Summer School, UEA Norwich. In 2020 she received first place in literature for the contest BiblioPrésVerts contest at Courmayeur, Region Valle d'Aosta, Italy, for her poetry, *La Sua Natura Recuperata*.

Studio Apartment: Eyrie

i.m. Lina Pancev[1]

The methods employed to ascend to the nest of a bird of prey
depend, in each instance, upon its site. If, however, the eyrie is
built in the fissure of a lofty rock, a man [already secured, with
such, as a rope] descends or is lowered from the rim of a mountain
or cliff to the level of the hollow in which the eyrie is built, and
[upon] entering, lifts the bird from the nest.

'How to reach the eyrie', *The Art of Falconry*, vol. 2 [2]

Naturally, he pursues me. In spite of, (or rather, more likely,
because of the lofty differences) – sex, age, class. Side effects no
doubt of the East-West détente. I am, after all, his *first girl*. To
reach me he will have to change territory, carry with him 'mon
adresse' turned 'il mio indirizzo' – a scrap of intemperance or
incitement that is surviving the creases it is folded under. As if
this wasn't enough, he must make enquiries. He has to climb,
in mean light, *five twisting flights*, of what has been condemned.
Traverse a banister *too shaky and broken to be depended upon*. He
does all this in spite.

Expecting no one, I was painting – a conspicuously clean portrayal
of a Venetian canal scene – my brush newly dipped, was hovering
just *out of the blue* paint tin, when the doorbell rang. 'Chi è?'
'It's me.' Ah, that English. I find him astonished, peering down
the sheer drop. I talk nonstop to relax him. Cook for us a simple
dinner: pasta, on the spirit stove, which is expressly forbidden.
But since when has propriety ever stopped me? I'm refusing to
pay rent, out of solidarity. What is important is that he has
desire. Above all, he is here. And from this vantage my life

is *a unique wonder that will never cease*. I am the fulcrum of this
fiction. I know this, instinctively – I say, *'I'm not in rivalry
never with no one.'* (My) Convictions usually arrive this way, a
stubborn bouquet of roses on a doorstep – unignorable, odious,
quasi-beautiful. *'Who sent these?'* Why? Probably, *a cavaliere.*
And furthermore, *who has horses in Venice to ride to the door?*
Fools, only the stubborn. Isn't it stubbornness that is keeping

me so girlishly young? My answer, 'He loves me.' (What more is
love than to be watched pacing the ground floor? To be dissident
to yourself, refugee in someone else?). I am not cruel

when I tell him, *'Go back to your own country'* and accompany
him down the precarious heights, carrying for us both some
precious little light.

---

[1] Lina Pancev, and all text in italics from *Territorial Rights* (1979) by Muriel Spark.
[2] 'How to reach the eyrie' in *The Art of Falconry*, volume 2, by Emperor Frederick II
of Hohenstaufen, ed. & tr. Casey Albert Wood and F. Marjorie Fyfe

Longways / Crosswise

poetry & dance sequence defining the Morecambe Bay passages

I

Definition /dɛfɪˈnɪʃ(ə)n/ [def-uh-nish-uh n] noun: the act of
defining; a statement expressing the essential nature of
something; clarity of visual presentation; distinctness of outline
or detail; sharp demarcation of outlines or limits

Longways /ˈlɒŋweɪz/ [lawng-weyz] adverb: along the length or
diagonally; a dance, usually folk, comprised of two straight lines

Crosswise /ˈkrɒswʌɪz/ [kraws-wahyz] adverb: so as to cross
something, from one side of a corner to another; at an angle; on
the bias; transversely; contrarily; obliquely

Passage /paˈsɑːʒ/ [pas-ij] noun: the action or process of moving
through or past somewhere on the way from one place to another;
the action or process of moving forward; a portion or section of
(written or artistic) work

Sequence /ˈsiːkw(ə)ns/ [see-kwuh ns] noun: a set of related
events, movements or items in succession; a continuous or
connected series

IV *Sea Calls Land / Land Calls Sea*

Dear Land – my devotion is shameless
pacing your outskirts, dirtying my dress
utterly consumed, humming oblivious
swish swish swish. I wish wish wish…
                                    – kiss kiss kiss

Dear Sea – you leave me with tide marks
I send messages with doves and skylarks.
No reply, save stillness or tempers. I miss
your swish swish swish. I wish wish wish…
                                    – kiss kiss kiss

VII *Lost*

Wait / something is out of place /
The hollow call of a bird migrated out
of season / a voice losing face in the fog /
pockets, threadbare unknowingly emptied /
the only silver lining, blown off course.
Too much salt in the heart, too much fog /
the mislaid gait of a spooked horse / settling
for doubt /not a single friend showing up /
the throat coarse, fraught, and not

                                    speaking out

VIII *In Fading Light (Coda)*
  for Ellen

However impossible, it is our nature to try,
        See? How the irides strive! Left hearted
and right minded, striving towards sight – striving
        the unmitigated bright, striving in fading light –

every 'aye', every eye, every I, tries… Oh, how we try!
        to comprehend the volumes in which we swim,
                and the heights that we breath in.

However improbable, it is in our nature to divine,
        to figure out the shadows.   See those
silhouettes, blithe against the sky?

Who are those slender waders? Numinous arquata,
messenger curlews, or the elusive sandpipers –
        mesmerising the unwary with their scintillating
                movements and wings like faeries?

However inconceivable, such Fairy Steps[3] exist –
        Dobbies[4] they will be, keepers of the shoreline
    nature spirits crossing over sands of time. *See?*

        How thought becomes manifest, how the I
continually tries every variation of light – every
        switch twitch glimpse means

wish wish wish
            wish   wish   wish
                wish   wish
                                        wish

---

[3] Fairy Steps refers to the medieval coffin route between Beetham, Arnside and Silverdale

[4] Dobbies are a type of fairy in folklore from England. In Lancashire any sort of outside ghost is called a dobby, and in Morecambe Bay they live along the shoreline. [Sources: Katharine Briggs, *An Encyclopaedia of Fairies* (1976), 103; Carol Rose, *Spirits, Fairies, Gnomes and Goblins* (1996), 88; Jacqueline Simpson & Stephen Roud, *A Dictionary of English Folklore* (2000).]

WARSAN SHIRE

Warsan Shire is a Somali British writer and poet born in Nairobi and raised in London. Her pamphlets, *Teaching My Mother How to Give Birth* (flipped eye, 2011) and *Her Blue Body* (flipped eye, 2015), were followed by her first book-length collection, *Bless the Daughter Raised by a Voice in Her Head* (Chatto & Windus, 2022), a Poetry Book Society Recommendation, which was shortlisted for the Forward Prize for Best First Collection. She was awarded the inaugural Brunel International African Poetry Prize in 2013 and served as the first Young Poet Laureate of London. In 2018 she became the youngest member of the Royal Society of Literature and is included in the Penguin Modern Poets series. Shire wrote the poetry for the Peabody Award-winning visual album *Lemonade* and the Disney film *Black Is King* in collaboration with Beyoncé Knowles-Carter. She also wrote the short film *Brave Girl Rising*, highlighting the voices and faces of Somali girls in Africa's largest refugee camp. Shire lives in Los Angeles with her husband and two children.

Backwards

The poem can start with him walking backwards into a room.
He takes off his jacket and sits down for the rest of his life,
that's how we bring Dad back.
I can make the blood run back up my nose, ants rushing into a hole.
We grow into smaller bodies, my breasts disappear,
your cheeks soften, teeth sink back into gums.
I can make us loved, just say the word.
Give them stumps for hands if even once they touched us without consent,
I can write the poem and make it disappear.
Step-dad spits liquor back into glass,
Mum's body rolls back up the stairs, the bone pops back into place,
maybe she keeps the baby.
Maybe we're okay, kid?
I'll rewrite this whole life and this time there'll be so much love,
you won't be able to see beyond it.

You won't be able to see beyond it,
I'll rewrite this whole life and this time there'll be so much love.
Maybe we're okay, kid,
maybe she keeps the baby.
Mum's body rolls back up the stairs, the bone pops back into place,
Step-dad spits liquor back into glass.
I can write the poem and make it disappear,
give them stumps for hands if even once they touched us without consent,
I can make us loved, just say the word.
Your cheeks soften, teeth sink back into gums,
we grow into smaller bodies, my breasts disappear.
I can make the blood run back up my nose, ants rushing into a hole,
that's how we bring Dad back.
He takes off his jacket and sits down for the rest of his life.
The poem can start with him walking backwards into a room.

Home

1

No one leaves home unless home is the mouth of a shark. You only run for the border when you see the whole city running as well. The boy you went to school with, who kissed you dizzy behind the old tin factory, is holding a gun bigger than his body. You only leave home when home won't let you stay.

No one would leave home unless home chased you. It's not something you ever thought about doing, so when you did, you carried the anthem under your breath, waiting until the airport toilet to tear up the passport and swallow, each mournful mouthful making it clear you would not be going back.

No one puts their children in a boat, unless the water is safer than the land. No one would choose days and nights in the stomach of a truck, unless the miles travelled meant something more than journey.

No one would choose to crawl under fences, beaten until your shadow leaves, raped, forced off the boat because you are darker, drowned, sold, starved, shot at the border like a sick animal, pitied. No one would choose to make a refugee camp home for a year or two or ten, stripped and searched, finding prison everywhere. And if you were to survive, greeted on the other side—*Go home Blacks, dirty refugees, sucking our country dry of milk, dark with their hands out, smell strange, savage, look what they've done to their own countries, what will they do to ours?*

The insults are easier to swallow than Ending your child's body in the rubble.

I want to go home, but home is the mouth of a shark. Home is the barrel of a gun. No one would leave home unless home chased you to the shore. No one would leave home until home is a voice in your ear saying—*leave, run, now. I don't know what I've become.*

II

I don't know where I'm going. Where I came from is disappearing. I am unwelcome. My beauty is not beauty here. My body is burning with the shame of not belonging, my body is longing. I am the sin of memory and the absence of memory. I watch the news and my mouth becomes a sink full of blood. The lines, forms, people at the desks, calling cards, immigration officers, the looks on the street, the cold settling deep into my bones, the English classes at night, the distance I am from home. Alhamdulillah, all of this is better than the scent of a woman completely on fire, a truckload of men who look like my father— pulling out my teeth and nails. All these men between my legs, a gun, a promise, a lie, his name, his flag, his language, his manhood in my mouth.

ROUND 1

ROWYDA AMIN

Rowyda Amin was born in Newfoundland, Canada to parents of Saudi Arabian and Irish origin, has lived in Riyadh and London, and is now based in New York City. Rowyda's poetry has appeared in two pamphlets, *Desert Sunflowers* (flipped eye) and *We Go Wandering at Night and Are Consumed by Fire* (Sidekick Books), in magazines including the *New England Review*, *The Poetry Review*, *Beloit Poetry Journal*, *Magma*, *swamp pink* and *Wasafiri*, and in anthologies including *Ten: new poets from Spread the Word* (Bloodaxe Books), *Lung Jazz: Young British Poets for Oxfam* (Cinnamon Press), *Bad Kid Catullus* (Sidekick Books), *Aquanauts* (Sidekick Books), *No, Robot, No!* (Sidekick Books), and *Bird Book: Towns, Parks, Gardens and Woodland* (Sidekick Books). She has performed her poetry at Ledbury Poetry Festival, Brighton Festival, the Victoria and Albert Museum and the Royal Festival Hall. Rowyda has won the Venture Award for poetry pamphlets from flipped eye publishing and the Queen Mary *Wasafiri* New Writing Prize for poetry. Her website is at www.rowyda. com.

Genius Loci

Rubbing my rhubarb in Washington Square, the infamous but
much-loved wearer of woollen hats in hot weather, the wonder
dog, lamper of gold-dust drudgers, champ of wild-goose pursuits,
I, (the one man band, clockless animal, whistling Tarzan), crap
in the grass, rapture dalliance on benches, chuckle in my yellow
beard a fuzz of tasty syllables. My drinking glass, my hand
I raise to Bird Man, pigeons on his shoulders, blues harp
in his lips to acclaim the wide-mouthed tulips' velveteen wine
and Kool-Aid hues; to bronze Giuseppe's pill-box, sarcastic
squirrels mocking tourists from on top; but not those green
Visigoths, the singalongers peddling gods. I'll take real figs
and not their painted ones. And you, stoic lunch-hour zebra
bent at your tuna sandwich, shrink-wrapped in pinstriped
wool for the daily auto-da-fé: do you question that I am cobalt
to the blood, a rain charmer, frog prince for a nickel with
cocksure loll, human with the composition of smoke? I shoulder
the kiloton of cogitation, the torture of dayglo tigers padding
nonstop my yellow sleeps; but to any tethered chimp that
pities me my leper life, I proffer this garden cosmopolis,
its stores of salt and creamsicle, lucid dreamers with eyes wide.

We Go Wandering at Night and Are Consumed by Fire

In the city are women with parchment faces,
with tree sap in their breasts,
who walk at night to pick pearl-light in the alleys.
Each window is a private theatre.
What shape behind the drapes?
Just the slender doctor passing between black tents
where no one has heard of religion
and knotweed binds the beds.
There is the mineral din
of children's bones growing in the night,

rubber seagulls on strings,
a shoal of black shoes in the river.
Glim of the gardens of Shalimar,
or else a bingo hall lit
with globes of grapefruit,
uranium glass hawked by kobold men
in the fog alleys,
in the tunnels of milk-white air.
The pigeons are jinx-carriers,
feathered with mirrorback silver
that catches the seconds on fire,
scatters light like the paper cells
where liquid turns to wasp.
I'm one in the crowd, at a time of fungible persons,
with the most advanced owlhead
antennae for looking backwards,
with a herbivore's instinct to flee
this fish-tank of portraits,
and a need to dance my shoes thin
before the stopper's set on the long bottle.
Water flows under the street
with a rattle of stray bones and keys.
Rain invites a murder of dark umbrellas.
I get lost in clouds of myself I meant crowds,
looking for my twin's dark hair
upside down in the black water.
Broken bulbs in the under-river tunnel.
On the bridge, people dancing,
moving like light against the rain's curtain.
Memorising trails of bitter almond,
how smoke in the trees makes bees heavy,
I smell caraway
on the moon's breath,
hear its antique neon buzz.
Tender vertebrae, a column of wet stone stairs,
leading to the cold hands
of men who have passed through
the revolving door of the river.
Their rook's-nest eyes,
their hair wax smelling of camphor,

beckonings
to their anaerobic palace of silt
with a whale skeleton as a ballroom
and promises of Roman beads,
a nixie's trousseau of indigo glass
and shards of Delft.
No, down there daylight
is a loose shake of pollen
from far banks of narcissus,
and I'd miss too much the cats' tails
forming question marks,
the lock-picking crows.
In the city, strange hearts tick
like bicycle wheels
through the lamplit forest.
Minds rustle, suitcases full of moths.
The wind makes a dirty oboe of the street,
notes grubby as lampblack,
sooty fingerprints.
From the statue of Hypnos,
monument to the inventor
of sleeping gas,
stragglers are chosen,
by boys dripping lice and pearls,
to be snared in alleys with moonlit
installations of mirrors.
The museum of the sarcophagus
and the mummified swan
is lulled
by black brambles
that hide its bricks.
Its sleeping rooms exhale
the scents of pepper
and thin grey amber,
distillates of furs
from deep attics.
They tremor
with the timbrels and bare
treading feet of the dancers
on the ancestral mandrake jars.

Inhaling vials of alkaline air,
I soar on glass propellers,
a night pollinator
guided by radio towers to spice islands
of tawny-bright music,

bowls of cognac and chloroform
stirred with roses,
ersatz orchestras in catacombs
linked by pneumatic tubes,
green-lit dives
where jellyfish faces bloom.
A midnight crowd shifts on insect pins
through pitchy vaults
and the smut-spore rain.
Night's mushroom scent:
old music, old lures,
labyrinths of the miniature.
At the sign of the Blue Lotus,
chlorophyll drips over sugar spoons.
Stirred fog, clouds
of water and anise,
lips brushed with tulip-feel.
Groping the wall marked with fox water,
where flowers phosphoresce between the cracks,
I find black honeycomb,
spiders trapped in jet.
The girls singing
from the throats of the oyster bed
tremor mercurial,
ointment that burns
with a blue flame when it's good.

MALIKA BOOKER

Malika Booker is a lecturer at Manchester Metropolitan University, a British poet of Guyanese and Grenadian Parentage, and co-founder of the writers' collective Malika's Poetry Kitchen. The anthology, *Two Young, Two Black, Too Different, Poems from Malika's Poetry Kitchen*, was published by Corsair to celebrate Malika Poetry Kitchen's 20th anniversary.

Her pamphlet, *Breadfruit* (flippedeye, 2007), was a Poetry Society Pamphlet Choice and her first book-length collection, *Pepper Seed* (Peepal Tree Press, 2013), was shortlisted for the OCM Bocas Prize for Caribbean Literature and for the 2014 Seamus Heaney Centre Prize for a first collection. She is published with the poets Sharon Olds and Warsan Shire in *Penguin Modern Poet Series 3: Your Family: Your Body* (2017). Booker and Shara McCallum recently co-edited an issue of *Stand* magazine curating an anthology of poems by African American, Black British, & Caribbean Women & Identifying Writers. Booker currently hosts and curates Peepal Tree Press's Literary podcast, *New Caribbean Voices*. A Cave Canem Fellow, and inaugural Poet in Residence at the Royal Shakespeare Company, Booker has received a Cholmondeley Award (2019) for outstanding contribution to poetry and was elected a Fellow of the Royal Society of Literature Fellow (2022). Her poem 'The Little Miracles', commissioned by and published in *Magma* 75 (autumn 2019), won the Forward Prize for Best Single Poem (2020).

Malika Booker's essay on the poem sequence which follows can be found on pages 194-204 of this book.

My Ghost in the Witness Stand

*   *   *

A Levite persuades his unlawful wife to return to him – JUDGES 19

(Objection)

- ·   The man raided like law was his warrant
- ·   What right to raid the law like his warrant, his right
- ·   The man persuaded/ raided/ marriage law his sanctity

Persuades
- Substitute dragged; hair clamped in palms
Persuades
- Substitute with hand collaring throat
Persuades
- Barricade breached, law unlawful to my body
Persuades
- His right, his might, my flight – ask why?
Persuades
- Picture fist hammering my cowering body, fake Tabanka smiles
Persuades
- Picture his smiles at wife with grilled teeth
Persuades
- Picture grip, and ignored, glass pressed into skin
Persuades
- Picture body in a car trunk
Persuades
- Picture body thrown, carted over donkey back
Persuade
- Picture punishable death.

*   *   *

This donkey can't drag no damn load.
This donkey can't drag no damn load.
This donkey can't drag no damn load.
The donkey can't drag no damn load.

This donkey can't drag no damn load.
This donkey can't drag no damn load.
This donkey can't drag no damn load.
This donkey can't drag no damn load.
This donkey can't drag no damn load.
This donkey can't drag no damn load.
This donkey can't drag no damn load.
This donkey can't drag no damn load.

This donkey can't drag no damn load.
This donkey can't drag no damn load.

*　　*　　*

And it came to pass in those days when
him woo me like dew shine on grass blade

And it came to pass in those days, when
I was pastures green, not ripe to be swayed

And that there was a certain Levite who look to him
steups – not took to him, state instead, 'ensnared'

And that there was a certain Levite who took to him…
that then wore, no, bruk me up like untamed mare

And that there was a certain Levite sojourning
loitering, liming to whistle gal passing rum shop

That there was a certain Levite sojourning
label horner man, who woo gal fi fling down hill top

Who took to him a concubine out of…
steups – say took me to him as damned wife thereof.

*　　*　　*

They have a way he start eye up my body
say he thickening me up like I is rump

    Say he thickening me up like I is rump
    body to disect, slaughter, quarter and cut up

Body to disect, slaughter, quarter and cut up
I was parade each day on   his auction block

    My parades are pirouettes, toes bloody on wood block
    is the way he watch me, make I had was to run

Is the way he fists lick me make I had was to run
one foot in front of the other, mi skin put foot

    One foot in front of the other, mi black skin put foot
    cos in his words I was a bird to pluck.

       *   *   *

Like yard fowl I run   run back   to mi Poopa   yard
but   but   he welcome   rancid as spoiled coconut
water.   *What mek yuh run, come back, home, little gal?*
over and   over like stuck record. When he   kick   kick
our dog down concrete steps.   When crushed   hibiscus
petals stained   stained our sheets   each morning's   bloom.
But was not poppa's bosom a rock and hard   hard chest!
His vile viper tongue hissed, *Sketel,*   hissed *salope,* said, *girl*
man have right to fling lash   in he wayward wife   ass
finger pointed   pointed   to St James scripture, like   Judge
verdict, then fist   hammered wood. Yet I know in these
island villages, when man shadow have weight heavy so,
is one sleep away from blood hot with rum   to raising cutlass,
over woman prone body, so I hauled up my skirt and put foot.

       *   *   *

he took a knife divided her together with her bones.
he took a knife divided her together with her bones.
he took a knife divided her together with her bones.
he took a knife divided her together with her bones.
he took a knife divided her together with her bones.
he took a knife divided her together with her bones.
he took a knife divided her together with her bones.
he took a knife divided her together with her bones.
he took a knife divided her together with her bones.
he took a knife divided her together with her bones.
he took a knife divided her together with her bones.
he took a knife divided her together with her bones.
he took a knife
he took a knife

JANET KOFI-TSEKPO

Janet Kofi-Tsekpo's work has been widely anthologised, and her chapbook *Yellow Iris* was published as part of the New-Generation African Poets series. She is currently undertaking a practice-based English and Humanities MPhil/PhD.

Yellow Iris

—sun's forgotten eye,
blinded,

hanging out
of earth's socket;

odourless
fen-filler,

corn crake feeder,
remedial beekeeper.

Self-seeding
invader

lining the riverbank,
swords high

under white heat.
Compass rose

at the margins,
flying the flag—

Streets

My sister and I were taken on one of our mother's rounds. We turned into a road with narrow houses on one side and prefab buildings on the other and, after knocking twice at one of the terraced houses, entered a dark room where a family sat inside. There was no buffer between the street and the living room, no double door or corridor through which we might enter. The family like the street were long and thin and grey, the husband a gaunt image of Mr Blunden, the mother's dead straight hair visibly thinning on top. They were related to some famous literary family; I don't remember which. The baby had been bitten by rats, and there were fears for the older child.

All through that summer,
sun rays smote the pavement
beyond the *dismal shade*.

The Wilton Diptych

The white hart's neck, divided
by crown and chain, merges again
with the gold sky, his head floating
above his body, the grass
near black in its midnight greenness.
The lion is fading now, his head
disappearing behind
the cracked canvas, though his tail
is strong. A deep red seeps
through the egg tempera.

MIR MAHFUZ ALI

Mir Mahfuz Ali was born in Dhaka, Bangladesh, and studied at Essex University. He dances, acts and has worked as a male model and a tandoori chef. He has given readings and performances at the Royal Opera House, Covent Garden, and other theatres in Britain and beyond. His poems have appeared in The Poetry Review, London Magazine, Poetry London, Ambit and PN Review. His first full-length collection, *Midnight, Dhaka*, was published by Seren in 2014. He was the winner of the 2013 Geoffrey Dearmer Prize for his poem, 'MIG-21 Raids at Shegontola', of which judge John Glenday said: 'Every effective poem works in a different way – each is a combination of craft, insight and imagination, but in Mir Mahfuz Ali's poem there is another ingredient – necessity. And by necessity I mean that quality which allows the poem to take a moral stance, to act as a redemptive force, rescuing the individual from history.' The poem was first published in *The Poetry Review*, 103:4, Winter 2013, edited by Maurice Riordan.

Isn't

Each time she spoke to me I felt myself
turning over to her. She and her rain-drenched
English land and language became one
and the same. It started out as a kiss
and what followed was much more than learning
the meaning of words written in her tongue.
I realised it was a serious affair,
and I'd never go back to my mother tongue
for nourishment again. It never struck me
switching one language for another
would make me a different person
and that I'd never get the old me back.

My lass was pleased with me, though
she knew I was imprecise and nicked words,
phrases, sentences from the silk-purse
of her mouth. When icy wind pierced my skin
I didn't complain. Instead, I built my fire
inside me, and began to import new sounds
into English. It was time we got married
but many whinged that a foreigner like me
was bound to corrupt their language,
and make it languorous rather than versatile.
They spat on my face for daring to build
a home in the beauty of their language.

My Salma

Forgive me badho, my camellia bush,
when you are full of yourself and blooming,

you may ask why, having spent so many years
comfortably in your breasts I still dream of Salma's,

just as I did when I was a hungry boy in shorts,
her perfect fullness amongst chestnut leaves.

The long grass broke as I ran, leaving
its pollen on my bare legs.

When the soldiers came, even the wind
at my heels began to worship Salma's beauty.

*

A soldier kicked me in the ribs. I fell
to the ground wailing.

They brought Salma into the yard,
asked me to watch how they would explode

a bullet into her. But I turned my head away
as they ripped her begooni blouse,

exposing her startled flesh. The young soldier
held my head, twisting it back towards her,

urging me to spit at a woman
as I might spit a melon seed into the olive dirt.

*

The soldier decorated with two silver bars
and two half-inch stripes was the first to drop his

ironed khaki trousers and dive on top of Salma.
His back arched as she fought for the last leaf

of her dignity. He laughed as he pumped
his rifle-blue buttocks in the Hemonti sun.

Then covered in Bengal's soft soil, he offered
her to the next soldier in line.

They all had their share of her,
dragged her away out of the yard.

I went in search of Salma,
amongst the firewood in the jungle.

*

Stood in the middle of a boot-bruised field,
working out how the wind might lead me to her.

Then I saw against the deepening sky
a thin mangy bitch, tearing at a body with no head,

breasts cut off in a fine lament,
I knew then who she was, and kicked

the bitch in the ribs, the same way
that I had been booted in the chest.

NICK MAKOHA

Nick Makoha is the founder of The Obsidian Foundation. Winner of the 2021 Ivan Juritz prize and the Poetry London Prize, he has been writer-in-residence for the ICA London and Wordsworth Trust. In 2017 his debut collection, *Kingdom of Gravity*, was shortlisted for the Forward Prize for Best First Collection and was a *Guardian* Best Book of the Year. Nick is a Cave Canem Graduate Fellow and won the 2015 Brunel International African Poetry Prize and the 2016 Toi Derricotte & Cornelius Eady Prize for his pamphlet *Resurrection Man*. His play *The Dark* – produced by Fuel Theatre and directed by JMK award-winner Roy Alexander – was toured nationally in 2019. It was shortlisted for the 2019 Alfred Fagon Award and won the 2021 Columbia International Play Reading Prize. His poems have appeared in the *Cambridge Review*, *The New York Times*, *The Poetry Review*, *The Rialto*, *Poetry London*, *TriQuarterly Review*, *5 Dials*, *Boston Review*, *Callaloo* and *Wasafiri*. He is a Trustee for the Arvon Foundation and the Ministry of Stories, and a member of the Malika's Poetry Kitchen collective. https://nickmakoha.com

Hollywood
Africans

The only thing that was certain was that it was June and
we had spilt a pepperoni pizza between us. An ultraviolet
light set the room. Basquiat channel surfing looking for
cartoons, while Icarus prodded a canvas to see if the image
fitted precisely in the frame. He was certain that someone
had broken in. I am getting set to coast towards the front
door when the girl of my dreams walks in. Now, I have to
make some lame excuse about how I'm off to the bodega
to get some smokes and how I have a craving for meat. I
am bound by this habit. She just smiles. I smile back. Then
a voice from the back of my throat says *you can come with*.
Cut to me and her at a stop sign. I don't want to play the
right game the wrong way. In the silence that has followed
us from the front door, I swat a crown of mosquitos above
her head. There is no water, but I can smell the ocean.
The man at the store is sweeping the street at which point
I ask her name. I have only ever seen her in a gallery with
a glass of prosecco in her hand. I watch the man watching
us in that night in that long summer. She pulls out some
ice cream from the freezer and adds it to the bill. The pulp
of her lips are flint and fire. The birds are silent and so is
the wind. The rest of the night falls away. In another magic,
she calls me by my original name. It is difficult to know
what to walk away from. She asks why my eyebrows are
raised. We are sitting on top of a park bench watching time.
We are a part of it, right here in New York City. This is
where the road delivers us towards the edge of difference.
Butterscotch drips from my fingers and falls to the tarmac.
A beautiful suspension. Then I or you or whoever decides
to look, hand-rolls a cigarette as we rummage through our
back pockets for a light.

Mecca

Downtown, summer lengthens. Basquiat starts painting
the never-ending night of space with its sonic madness
as if it were water flowing down to the sea. The poet exits
the subway to enter the gallery. In the basement, he salutes
the painter with the words Spirit and Fire. Which loosely
translates to – Forgive this interlude.[1] I've never been able
to find a recording of President[2] Johnson signing the Treaty
on the Non-Proliferation of Nuclear Weapons. Outside my
apartment window, a patch of grass is trying to become
a desert.[3] I bet you with sweat dripping down his back
after making love to his wife in the Oval office Johnson
realises that if he lets them push the button then his grandchildren
won't survive. And that's why he signs. Because Mrs Johnson
won't be able to conceive.[4] Or maybe as the barber wraps
a hot towel around his face[5] – the same intimacy men have
when they prepare their parachutes to jump out of a plane,
the same intimacy[6] devoid of the moon.[7] Maybe, by the process
of elimination, this is how things disappear.[8] But if the plane
disappears what happens to the hostages?[9] Scratch that!

---

[1] Scratch that!

[2] Scratch that!

> [3] Scratch that!

> [4] Scratch that!

[5] – in that intimacy

> [6] that Rameses II hand maidens wrapped
> his body as they hummed his name in a sky
> [7] Or his name, that was sugar water in their mouth,
> as they massaged the bones of the great hidden God.
> [8] If the oceans disappear it will invite the sun to its house?
> [9] If Amin disappears who will look after my people.
> Could you love my city as if it were your own?

143

A True Account[1]

JFK   LAX to JFK. A warrior wind is seeking what we have lost
but the pilot has the wings of the redeye under his
command. As the night flickers on – The world

below widens – bat-like[2] – I wonder what the night sees in
me – A thing that flies from earth to pour its pain into an
island smaller than this one – You

don't always get the story you want even when the runway
changes – Once, in a type of beginning, after The Roots
concert but before check-in – I packed

my bag the way I pack my heart – There it lay on the bed
– towel around my waist – At check-in, the stewardess
with perfect posture handed me back my

passport as if it were weightless[3] – Actually, more than
once I have packed my heart in a bag hoping that it could
inhabit a body/memory/island bigger

than this one – If I stay still for too long the body hardens
the way that black cake does when you don't follow the
recipe[4] – Dear friends, although I pick

at my lunch it does not alter the natural order of things –
This flight bears the sweetness of wings[5] but it is not a
cure for exile – If I were to say how much

further? – it would make no difference – As we descend
toward the shoreline, read my eyes like a clock – surely
the sky in its appetite is open to us?

¹ of a Hijacking at Entebbe Airport

² It begins with a slogan like *The City Never Sleeps* and a descending prayer call whispering in the wind and an idea that works – entrusted to the bodyguard at the temple – as a people attempt to become a modern imperial state. Now, whether they will succeed will depend on how they enter the next scene. Ammunition prices have risen dramatically. In an upswept house a woman enters from the street outside with her first-born cradled in her arms. Her streets like mine are filled with security-men with old rifles.

³ Does that make us kin? She uncovers her face and shuts the rest of the world out. This is what I have learnt, the man who sleeps in her bed will be dead in week. Unlike Ulysses he will not come home from the war. When the space his heart takes becomes a leaking red dot, she will swear she saw his face in the clouds. Women will think she is talking to the sun (whose power it is to make the gods afraid) with its red centre. For a while they will entertain it when she writes in the sand – *I have watched over you*.

⁴ But this is not the Shield of Achilles or the Star of David. When beetles see its glow, they run backward into the dark. What is the purpose of an empty field? Mr Cain, my science teacher, would look me in the face as if the boats were coming in and say – *A field is a numerical property of an extended part of the universe*. The smart Alec in me would ask – Do you know how to get there from here? My family picked cotton in a field. Here – a dark sky. There is an airfield. He – who she calls her shield – has now a battered body.

⁵ Dear circus, dear night of the blooming flower, dear dark sky, and dear country to which I have not returned, dear thought in which the vinegar of my conscious swims – take me back to the cockpit and the pilot with a gun pointed to his head. Why does he not break loose when he and his crew are offered freedom? Instead, in the weight of that dimension, he says words that like twilight are worth repeating – What I am is not important. And in that delicate frequency with lowered guns, they give him back his life.

SHAZEA QURAISHI

Shazea Quraishi is a Pakistani-born Canadian poet and translator based in London. A selection of her work was included in the Bloodaxe anthology *Ten: new poets from Spread the Word* in 2010 and her first pamphlet, *The Courtesans Reply*, was published by flipped eye in 2012. *The Art of Scratching*, her first book-length collection, was published by Bloodaxe Books in 2015. Her second, *The Glimmer*, followed from Bloodaxe in 2022.

She runs regular workshops through *Poetry Studio: at home in the world* – a hospitable online space for new and experienced poets to come together to read poems in English and in translation, to inspire writing in session. A tutor with the Poetry School and RHACC School of Ideas, she is a senior writer in residence with Living Words, an arts charity working in creative partnership with people impacted by dementia or mental health concerns. She is a trustee on the board of English PEN, and on the committee of the Poetry and Spoken Word Group of the Society of Authors.

The Taxidermist attends to her work[1]

A white mouse (2)

what has a white mouse to show us

I meet him
white   mute   item

    (fate
    air hums with it)

he was
he is

    I sew him shut
    wish him home

Mexican mouse opossum

supine campesino
no nip no pounce no noise
                suspense

someone's cousin
        compassion comes

I coax   ~~escape?~~   ~~séance?~~
a sepia pause
immense comma

Volcano rabbit

torn bobtail
no antic

    coat
        tail
            rib

    coral ribbon alit

vacant aria
a volt into air

[1] The taxidermy poems employ an anagram form inspired by the French post-surrealist group OULIPO (Ouvroir de Littérature Potentielle), a gathering of mathmeticians, scientists and writers who embrace constraint as a means of triggering ideas and inspiration.

[2] Susana Chávez Castillo (November 5, 1974 – *c*. January 6, 2011) was a Mexican poet and activist who led protests against the violent killings of women in Ciudad Juárez since the 1990s. She coined the phrase 'Ni una muerta más' – 'Not one more woman dead' – which was used at protests, and she took part in poetry readings that she dedicated to the murdered women. She was brutally murdered in 2011.

In the branches of your voice

by SUSANA CHÁVEZ CASTILLO[2]

Light, unquestioning, keeps vigil,
and your eyes open forever.
I'm speaking of the heart faced with death
in the branches of your voice,
with one lip of earth, and another of night,
with a heart of dust, and another of wind.

I'm speaking of this love
this navigating through fog,
this love, this love.

Each silence brings us to the word that reflects us –
your loneliness takes shape within my body,
and stars crumble in your absent gaze.

Sometimes I find you in a face you never had,
in a ghostly form you didn't deserve,
and silence raises its head to look at me.
This time we return at night –
trees hold on to their birds
and tiredness extends its tongue to sing in our ears.

Night arrived in your heart,
and your eyes closed as the world entered.

And yet, somehow, we all knew,
and something now breaks memory in two.
Something breaks in two the woman who combs her soul
before entering her narrow bed,
and the night,
like a glass that falls from the hand of a frightened child,
breaks in two.
Something already broken, breaks in two.

translated by Shazea Quraishi

En el árbol de la voz
by SUSANA CHÁVEZ CASTILLO[2]

A ciegas la luz vela
y unos ojos se abren para siempre.
Hablo del corazón frente a la muerte,
en el árbol de la voz, con un labio de tierra y otro
de noche,
con un corazón de polvo y otro de viento.

Hablo de este amor,
esta navegación entre la bruma,
este amor, este amor.

Cada silencio nos llevará a la palabra que nos refleja,
y en mí toma cuerpo tu soledad,
en tu mirada ausente se deshacen los astros.

A veces te descubro en el rostro que no tuviste,
en la aparición que no merecías.
Y el silencio levanta la cabeza y me mira.
Esta vez volvemos de noche,
los árboles han guardado sus pájaros,
el cansancio estira su lengua para cantarnos al oído.

La noche llegó en tu corazón,
tus ojos se cerraron en la llegada del mundo.

Y sin embargo, de alguna manera, todos lo sabíamos,
y algo parte en dos la memoria,
algo parte en dos a la mujer que peina su alma antes
de entrar al lecho solitario,
y parte también el tiempo de la noche,
como el vaso que cae de la mano de algún niño asustado,
algo parte en dos lo que estaba partido.

ROGER ROBINSON

Roger Robinson is a writer who has performed worldwide. He is the winner of the T.S. Eliot Prize 2019 and RSL Ondaatje Prize 2020, and an FRSL. He was chosen by Decibel as one of 50 writers who have influenced the Black British writing canon. His latest collection *A Portable Paradise* was a *New Statesman* Book of the Year. His collections have been shortlisted for the OCM Bocas Poetry Prize and the Oxford Brookes Poetry Prize, commended by the Forward Poetry Prize and shortlisted for the Derek Walcott Prize for Poetry 2020. He has received commissions from the National Trust, London Open House, BBC, National Portrait Gallery, Victoria & Albert Museum, INIVA, MK Gallery and Theatre Royal Stratford East where he also was an associate artist.

He is an experienced workshop leader who has toured extensively with the British Council. His workshops have been part of a shortlist for the Gulbenkian Prize for Museums and Galleries and were also a part of the Webby Award winning Barbican's *Can I Have a Word*. He is co-founder of both Spoke Lab and the international writing collective Malika's Poetry Kitchen. He is the lead vocalist and lyricist for King Midas Sound and has also recorded solo albums with Jahtari Records.

Halibun for the Onlookers

The people on the ground look up at the burning building,
their faces illuminated by the glow of fire-ash floating gently down.
Pieces of burning building fall like giant sparks from a welder's torch,
then a flaming fire-snake slides its way from the fourth floor
straight to the top. In the lights from mobile phones,
shadows wave makeshift flags, until they no longer wave them
and their silhouette fades to the roaring fiery light.

The spectacle's now more like a painting of a building on fire than
an actual fire: black velvet night rippling orange-yellow and punch-
red acrylic flames.

The lookers are imagining their settees in flames, their orange floral
wallpaper slowly bubbling up and bursting like blisters before giving
in to a blackened charred heat. Then the swan dive of a few bodies.
Some sob for their own, some sob for others, some just sob.
The soot in the air burns in the noses of onlookers. Smoke makes
some wheeze in the branched bronchiole of their lungs, from when
they were in the building, then not totally on fire, but from corridors
of smoke, when they edged blindly towards the stairwell, hoping not
to walk into fire.

The sky's darker now as background to the flame,
the smoke rising like an offering of burning sage.
The building has become a charred black tomb,
and the sky looks down on us saying what's lost is lost,
gather what is left and build new lives.

As for the onlookers, whose numbers have swelled, this is what they'll
remember: the floating ash and flaming debris, bodies in flight and
bodies in shadow, the smoke leaving discreetly into the night sky,
clouds at night and the snake, the giant snake of flaming fire.

The heat at my back,
I throw my baby out the window.
Catch him Lord!

Woke

I woke up in chains in the belly of the slave ship. The dip of the bow and the moan of the timbers made me fall asleep. When I woke again I was being whipped to get up. I passed out and when I woke I was on an auction block as men with ashy fingers checked my teeth. With a neck iron digging into my skin, I walked till I collapsed and when I woke the neck iron had become a noose which they pulled until I choked. I saw them looking at me, even little white kids pointing till it all went black. I woke up being sprayed to the floor with police hoses and dogs snapping at my shins. As the dog sank its teeth in my calf, a police hit me with his baton until I passed out. I woke up on the 16th floor of a tower block looking out the window with a clear view of the land that does not belong to me.

Lisbon

I was on holiday with my girlfriend in Lisbon, I was on a bus full of black Portuguese passengers. I listened and then I realised that I could understand all the conversations. Gossip about boyfriends, anger with bosses, information about stopping irritation, laments that the driver was driving too slow. I thought that they all knew English and it slowly dawned on me that they were all speaking Portuguese. I don't speak Portuguese but I could understand every word. I told my girlfriend that I could understand every word the Portuguese bus goers were saying; but she couldn't understand me and as she spoke I couldn't understand her. I thought that perhaps I was too tired from the plane flight but my comprehension continued and my girlfriend was getting frustrated thinking that I was faking it somehow. I asked a black man in Portuguese if he spoke English to translate between my girlfriend and I. He said yes. I explained the situation to him. He looks at me for a second and says it in English to my girlfriend.

My girlfriend shouts something to me and storms off. I look at him and ask what did she say? He averts his eyes and says he'd rather not say

Returnee

After more than two decades abroad he returned to Brixton. The reggae shop where he used to buy mixtapes straight from Jamaica has become a gluten-free muffin shop. The market where he used to buy red snapper is now a burger joint where the burgers cost ten pounds with an extra pound for ketchup. The market is now full of exotic meats: Octopus, Manta Ray, *something* gamey called Buffalypso. It's the pace he misses most, everything seems slowed down, a pace designed for leisure, not culture. No more could he revel in its energy, its frenetic pace. The store signs are less crowded with fonts, and each one is in Farrow & Ball colours, no hard primary colour contrasts, everything muted and lacking in black aesthetics. Chosen for statement not attention. For a minute he thought that he'd seen a Caribbean food place like the ones he was used to, but as he got closer the interior was meant as a kitsch statement of times past, and it was vegetarian. The barbershop had become a second-hand art bookshop, the greasy spoon had become a cheese and champagne shop. He went back to his boutique hotel on Electric Avenue and asked the receptionist where he could find a few simple things like a beef patty and some peanut punch. The receptionist told him that he wouldn't get that anywhere around here, but that she could bring some in for him when she came in to work tomorrow.

Blood

That was the decade of black blood, so much blood they couldn't contain it. It overflowed from baths, pots and pans outdoors, down streets, down drains. Cars started to float away, buses turned over and the people and families had to tread blood, as some people drowned in it. So much black blood. Black people stood on roofs to escape drowning in it. The helicopters flew like giant flies around the bloodied buildings. People waved flags hoping that they'd be saved. Then it dawned on them that the helicopters weren't there to save them. The helicopters were there to watch them. To observe them and their blood. They could smell the blood's meaty rotting stench from high up in the air; they could see the houses being swallowed in red. And that's what we saw on TV, on mobile phones, on our computer screens being filled up with red, more red and nothing but red black blood.

DENISE SAUL

Denise Saul's debut collection *The Room Between Us* (Pavilion /
Liverpool University Press, 2022) was shortlisted for the T.S.
Eliot Prize 2022, longlisted for the Jhalak Prize 2023, and was
a Poetry Book Society Recommendation. She is the author of
two pamphlets: *White Narcissi* (flipped eye, 2007), a Poetry
Book Society Pamphlet Choice; and *House of Blue* (Rack
Press, 2012), a PBS Pamphlet Recommendation. A recent
guest editor of *The Poetry Review*, Denise is a past winner of
the Poetry Society's Geoffrey Dearmer Prize and is a judge
for the T.S. Eliot Prize 2023. She holds a PhD in Creative
Writing (poetry) from the University of Roehampton. She
received an ACE Grant for the Arts Award for her video poem
collaborative project, *Silent Room: A Journey of Language* (see
silent-room.net). Born and raised in London, she lives in Surrey.

The Room Between Us

There you are, beside the telephone stand,
waiting for me in a darkened room
when I force open the white door.
There you lie, behind it.

I never found out why you grabbed
a pewter angel instead of the receiver
when you tried to call me that morning.
I give up trying to lift you from the floor

as the room is no longer between us.
You point again to the Bible, door, wall
before I whisper, *It's alright, alright,*
now tell me what happened before the fall.

A Daughter's Perspective

When morning arrives, the radio stops speaking. Now, instead of hearing my mother speak from one, infinitely distant (and divine) point of view, further points of view are included in our conversation.

If I stand in front of the window and look at her wheelchair, the person in front of me seems to be smaller the closer she is.

I rub handcream into the back of her hand, starting at the wrist and working away from the heart. The nurse told me that it was better to massage away from the heart and not towards it. My mother opens her left hand and I pour some cream in her palm. She massages the back of my hand. I talk to her about work, neighbours and when she would be coming home.

A representation of a scene is often one simple conversation.

I asked the physiotherapist about walking with a cane. In the beginning, I thought she said that walking was possible. Even though I asked her before about leg supports, she said *never* and *wheelchair*. But since my question did not produce an answer, I repeated it. She stood still looking around the room as though she had never been here. On the second visit, I did not expect an answer from her because I had asked the same question twice.

In the evening, I read Paul Broca's *Mémoires d'Anthropologie*. My mother recites sentences from the left hemisphere: *In the mindfulness of listening, Sundays at home at home.*

Stone Altar

I am not sure how the stone travelled
from British Guiana but the story goes
my mother brought it to England to remind her
of a passing like the way one remembers
the flight of a bird by keeping its feather.
What I thought was limestone was chalk
passed down from grandmother Frances
found among other stones in a black handbag
pushed to the back of a cabinet.
That autumn I asked my sister to tell me about
the stone when I sifted through the possessions.
When chalk gave away some dust, she held it
up to the light and told me about
other things in a world of decay.
It seemed easy enough for her to
wipe away the dust from her fingers.
No one receives what they truly want.
It took me a while to understand all of this
when I placed the chalk on an altar
next to blue kyanite stones I collected.

Golden Grove

i.m. Aubrey

Unbearable as night from which sleep comes,
you are everywhere at once: in the wind
on sunken earth   in stilling water.
I carry your heavy urn to Golden Grove
where tamarind trees emerge as woods.

The dream holds back day from night.
And you, a wanderer, could not wait
to leave rain behind in our city.
You will now become a thousand things:
scent of jasmine   salted air   troubling light.

SENI SENEVIRATNE

Born in Leeds and currently living in Derbyshire, Seni is a writer of English and Sri Lankan heritage, published by Peepal Tree Press. Her books include *Wild Cinnamon and Winter Skin* (2007), *The Heart of It* (2012), and *Unknown Soldier* (2019), inspired by her father's experience as a signalman in the Second World War, which was a Poetry Book Society Recommendation, a National Poetry Day Choice and highly commended in the Forward Poetry Prizes 2020. Her fourth collection, *The Go-Away Bird*, is published by Peepal Tree in 2023. She is co-editor, with Shash Trevett and Vidyan Ravinthiran, of the anthology *Out of Sri Lanka* (Bloodaxe Books, 2023). Her work has been widely published in several anthologies and magazines, most recently in *100 Queer Poems* (Penguin), *Where We Find Ourselves* (Arachne Press) and *Wretched Strangers* (Boiler House Press), *The Rialto* and *New England Review*. She has collaborated with filmmakers, visual artists, musicians and digital artists, and is one of ten commissioned writers on the Colonial Countryside Project. She is currently working on an LGBTQ project with Sheffield Museums entitled *Queering the Archive*.

Lightkeeping

You might be surprised to learn
it was an oak tree that inspired
the engineer who built the lighthouse
on Eddystone Rocks in 1756 –
a discovery I make on a trawl
through Wikipedia, which takes me
as far back as 279 BC where Pharos,
the first recorded lighthouse, stood
in Alexandria harbour and survives,
beyond the earthquakes that destroyed it,
in *phare*, *faro*, *farol*, *far* – the way words
heard and carried home by travellers
can often merge with other tongues.

My journey takes me to the 18th century,
to be told how the building of lighthouses
'boomed in lockstep with burgeoning levels
of transatlantic…'
and here I am stopped short because
there is something about the word
transatlantic that never fails to lurch me
into the hold of a ship. I never intended
when I began, to end up here but this
is how it works when everything seems
to be drenched in that particular history
which is why, right now, I need to know
if any oak-shaped towers were beacons
for the ships of traders and by virtue of that
(though vice would be more appropriate)
were complicit in the trafficking of people.
I've no wish to implicate the lightkeepers
in all this, since they were in their own way
fodder for the traders' profits – the details
of which, I had intended to write about:
how they'd keep the lamps burning and
work sixteen-hour shifts so you'd hear
the foghorn's earsplitting warning, even if
you couldn't see beyond the end of your nose.

The Devil's Rope

I

Devil knows I've mauled a good few bodies
in my day and often left the souls for him.
Lock-out? Lock-in? Moot point and makes no odds.
Whatever way you cross, I'll cut your skin
but still you try to dodge my barbs, poor sods.
I've crossed the open plains and closed them in,
I've edged a Desert War, I've manned the trenches.
Now I'm raising Fortress Europe's latest fences.

II

A pioneer in 1871,
I was proud to be the settlers' solution.
Who cared if tribal ways of life were gone
now that the buffalo would face extinction.
Don't blame me – a mere pawn in Lincoln's plan
to span from coast to coast and build a nation.
He left the Sioux and Cheyenne with no hope –
I guess that's why they named me 'Devil's Rope'.

My exploits in the trenches made me famous,
I thrived in war, I stood up to the test.
I'm proud to say my presence made men nervous.
My coils were sharp. Troops fell. You know the rest.
I'll tell you, at the risk of sounding callous,
I served both sides and always did my best
to shield them, but my main aim was to rip.
So countless soldiers died whilst in my grip.

I did the job so well they brought me back
for World War Two. Ideal for desert duty,
on Rommel's frontline against the Desert Rats,
I travelled north from Sollum over thirty
sandy miles to Jaghboub. Hard to keep track
of all my talents, all my dirty tricks.
One thing is clear, I'm keen to serve, upstanding.
To tell the truth, I don't care who's commanding.

I'm not done yet. Now Europe needs defence.
It's not my fault if children get entangled
in my razor wiring. There's no pretence
the work is tough, seen from any angle,
no matter their distress, I am the fence
that holds Europe's borders. Let's not wrangle.
Though refugees deserve the chance to settle,
I thwart their hopes – proving the strength of metal.

The Weight of the World

Oh, how they blew like vast sails in the breeze,
my mother's wet sheets, pegged hard to the rope
of her washing line. There was always hope
of dry weather and no need for a please
or thanks between us as we hauled them down.
Whether to make the fold from right to left
or left to right, to tame the restless heft?
My job to know. I won't call it a dance
but there were steps to learn and cues to read,
the give and take of fabric passed like batons
in a relay race. She was my due north.
Her right hand set west, mine tracing the east,
we closed the distance, calmed the wayward weight,
bringing order to the billowing world.

KAREN McCARTHY WOOLF

Born in London to English and Jamaican parents, Dr Karen McCarthy Woolf, FRSL, is the author of two poetry collections and the editor of seven literary anthologies and numerous journals. Shortlisted for the Forward Felix Dennis and Jerwood Prizes, her debut *An Aviary of Small Birds* tells the story of losing a son in childbirth and was an *Observer* Book of the Year. Her latest, *Seasonal Disturbances*, explores gentrification, the city and the sacred, and was a winner in the inaugural Laurel Prize for ecological poetry and excerpted in *The Financial Times* and *The Guardian*.

In 2019 she moved to Los Angeles as a Fulbright Postdoctoral Scholar and Writer in Residence at the Promise Institute for Human Rights at UCLA, exploring the relationship between poetry, law and capitalism's impacts on Black, brown, indigenous and working-class bodies. She returned to the UK before embarking on a fellowship at the Sacatar Institute in Brazil where her research focused on sugar and its material and cultural legacies.

Karen has performed her work at literature festivals worldwide – in Mexico, Trinidad, Jamaica, Italy, America and China at venues including the Royal Festival Hall, Barbican and King's Place for Poetica Electronica, which showcased music collaborations with various dance and techno producers. Her poems have been translated into Turkish, Swedish, Spanish, Polish and Dutch, produced as animated and choreographed short film, exhibited by Poems on the Underground and dropped from a helicopter over the Houses of Parliament in a poetry 'bombing'.

Karen currently teaches at Goldsmiths College, University of London, writes poetry criticism and has served on the judging panels of numerous prizes including the Brunel International African Poetry Prize, the National Poetry Competition and the Forward and Gingko Prizes. Her hybrid verse novel *Top Doll* is forthcoming from Dialogue Books in 2024.

Excerpts from Un/Safe

*   *

On our road trip from Wyoming to Colorado via South
Dakota I notice the animals, the cattle are all more tightly
penned, squashed together like marshmallows in a packet,
though deer still run at the edge of the fence. We've been
in Nebraska two minutes when the police pull us over.
The younger officer is the Sheriff. He's nervous. Terribly
polite. Introduces himself. As Rhett. *Not Rhett Butler* he
says. But it is like Rhett Butler. It is a gleaming, multi-
columned southern mansion. Especially when he laughs,
nervously, did I say that he was nervous? Did I say the
older officer never takes his hand off his gun? Won't look
me in the eye? Keeps his distance. That I'm careful to
move slowly as I reach into the glove compartment for
Zoë's papers? Did I say that Zoë is dark skinned? *Can you
imagine a* whiter *name?* Rhett asks.

*   *

* *

O England, boasted land of liberty,
With strangers still thou mayst thy title own
But thy poor slaves the alteration see
With many a loss to them the truth is known

JOHN CLARE, 'The Village Minstrel'

O England, boasted land of liberty

     Of palms drummed strong on pink & gristled chests
     Of lawns landscaped to rust, liverish
           as dogs' piss in summer's drought, windswept

& observed on closed & uptight circuits
— where one good eye's enough. How erotic!

       Always to be watched, while we slept
through hurricanes & other chaotic
             procedures.

Our demise a triptych
on the walls of multi-storey, glassy cathedrals:
the centre panel a tissue of idyllic
hills & hens clucking a corporate pastoral,

epic as it was causal.

On every treetop a crow, crowned
        a survivor, guzzling from oily puddles
while worthless Kings   allowed
Nothing & Everything
       so kleptocracy flowered
bloody as exploded capillaries*

     *exponential detonations designed to devour
     all forms of flesh & resistance, bodily
     or otherwise.

O Walled World of disparity
                & hard surfaces—
Of barbed
      fences augmented by engineered despair
      & steel cages.
Where algorithmic swords
      pierce skin, gluttonous for the gruel of hard knocks.

Behold the petal, silky & violet!

      Only bees ignore the buzz
      of armed response:
             systems to keep each Eden inviolate.

Every lavender bush & cactus flower is private.
Do not pick the fruit! A pilfered blackberry
is a sin that stains this age of ordered disquiet.
In America, O, boasted land of liberty!

O boasted land of liberty, America!
      Of winged flamingo skies & thrusting palms
      Of sweat-rich fields & manufactured terror
deadly as Academy Awarded Napalm
      (don't forget the TMs —)

for nouns & verbs can be bought & loaned
& although the Enemy is History, mis/remembered:
             With strangers still thou may thy title own.

You claim these stolen lands, call elders Crone
& daughters Bitches.
           As if the one who calls you friend
deserves no more than scorn.
Who doesn't need a bone
to chew on—?

God knows why else a dog still loves a fiend.
Blood rules the pack that blindly
follows, nose to the coiled & entrailed end.

     —But thy poor slaves the alteration see.

Tents deemed to have marred
the view are removed:
residents gunned down
when they protest against hostile fire.

    With many a loss to them the truth is known.

NATHALIE TEITLER

Nathalie has worked promoting diversity in literature for over 20 years and was named an Honorary Fellow of the RSL. She ran the Complete Works Poetry, founded by Bernardine Evaristo, OBE, from 2008 to 2020. Prior to that she ran the first national mentoring and translation programme at Exiled Writer Ink. She also founded *Dancing Words*, an organisation producing dance poetry films and events. The films have been shown at the BFI, Tate, Southbank Centre and at festivals around the world. In 2020 she edited the anthology *Un Nuevo Sol: British Latinx Writers* (flipped eye), the first major anthology of Latinx writers in the UK that had international success. She runs the organisation of the same name with the award-winning poet/translator Leo Boix and writer and Director of the Forward Foundation, Mónica Parle. *Un Nuevo Sol* nurtures British Latinx writers and builds bridges with Latinx and Latin American writers throughout the world through short films, translations, collaborations, cross-art events and more. Nathalie was born in Buenos Aires and holds a PhD in Latin American poetry (King's College London, 2000). She is currently working on a novel celebrating the extraordinary world of tango in 1900.

ESSAYS

RAYMOND ANTROBUS

Bird Song and Resonance

Where are the songs of Spring? Ay, where are they?

JOHN KEATS

A few years ago, a study at King's College London suggested that city-dwellers who live in close proximity to birds, birdsong, trees and sky are happier than those that don't. I think about this often, because I don't hear birdsong unless I have my hearing aids in: their calls are too shrill and high pitched for my unaided ears. It was one of the most striking sounds to me when I was first fitted with hearing aids at seven years old. In an old poem of mine, titled 'The First Time I Wore Hearing Aids' I describe how the 'pigeon-flapping, crowded city traffic avalanched my ears like never before'. Could this new access to sound improve my chances of a happier life?

In 2020 I moved from London to live in Oklahoma City with my wife, Tabitha. The pandemic had shut the immigration offices, halting the process of our marriage visa for nine lonely and frustrating months. She had to return to the US because she'd lost her right to a work visa, which meant I had to follow her wherever she could find work. I was reluctant to go: All I knew about Oklahoma was from media consumption: The Oklahoma bombing, cowboys and Republicans.

But I found myself living with Tabitha in a large, red-bricked house with a lawn and a driveway, looking out onto a wide open green park full of trees and grass green space with a narrow stream running through the middle of it. There were squirrels, raccoons and possums staggering around. We also lived by two tornado sirens, which occasionally rang out, a long droning sound that echoed for miles like the blarings that were heard in London during the Blitz. Ralph Ellison was born near the house we

173

ended up renting. The local library was named in his honour. This comforted me, gave me a map of literary territory to ground myself.

In a 1961 interview, Ralph Ellison was asked about his Oklahoma City upbringing. He described himself as 'of the city' because he didn't share the agricultural experiences of many of his classmates who were born on farms. He explained that the state was open to American settlers in 1889, with Ellison being born seven years after that. Oklahoma (at this point) had no tradition of slavery, which created fluidity between black and white races. His parents had left the city of Georgia before he was born, seeking a broader freedom than was offered black people anywhere else in America at that time.

Each morning Tabitha and I would walk around the park before work. At this point in time, Oklahoma had one of the highest Covid rates in the US. Trump was running for re-election and the air everywhere felt hardened by uprisings following the murder of George Floyd. We saw as many Trump rallies as we saw Black Lives Matter demonstrations.

Yet, within this open green space Tabitha and I found ourselves between the noise. We got to know some of the locals: The friendly dog-walking neighbours called the neighbourhood 'the blue bubble', within it I was the right kind of outsider: a married, mild mannered, English-speaking British poet.

Before people heard my voice they often thought I was Latinx or indigenous. Oklahoma has the third biggest indigenous population in the United States.

Because of the way the land is historically divided and an enduring indigenous population, people aren't pushed onto reservations in the same way that is usually the case in North America. Much of the land is legally acknowledged as indigenous land, the largest being the Cherokee Nation of Oklahoma. It's complicated, much of this has to do with the aftermath of The Trail of Tears, the American Civil war and the complex integration of federal and tribal law. From this legal perspective, whose land is whose is still largely contested.

At the entrance to the Oklahoma Contemporary museum, where Tabitha worked, you're greeted with a land acknowledgement that states 'We honour the indigenous people who inhabited these lands before the United States was established. Today, 39 distinct tribal nations reside in Oklahoma.'

Jonny, a colleague of Tabitha's in the contemporary art centre, was a bald slick stocky man who wore small black bowler hats, chunky silver rings, a perfectly trimmed moustache that arched his mouth and tribal tattoos on each arm. He used to pull up outside our house, each time in a different vehicle (each engine louder than the other) a truck, a motorbike, a sports car; the birds fluttering from the trees with each visit. Jonny introduced me to Oklahoma City nightlife, driving me to bars and roadside food stops, *'AY! MY BOY IS A WRITER!'* he bellowed in the bar one night, 'HE *GOT BOOKS WITH HIS NAME ON IT AN' SHIT!'*, Jonny's friends gathered around me, offering drinks, prompting questions about London and my Oklahoma hot takes. '*Man,*' I said, standing by the fire pit in the beer garden, '*it's lockdown so I haven't seen much, but I like it, man, as long as it's calm.*' Each of Jonny's friends would offer a site, somewhere I should check out for scenic reasons, a highway I should drive across, a lake during a sunset, or a particular field during a sunrise.

The opposite of Jonny was Pablo; he was also one of Tabitha's colleagues at the local museum, a tall brown man with long Indian hair, a pressed suit and smooth clean-cut jaw. His face was friendly, I found myself smiling in his presence, even when he was silent or pausing between words, his demeanour inspired patience, a calming wholesomeness. Many of his stories and anecdotes involved the animal world.

Disclaimer, I'm about to tell a story about an owl. Owls are considered sacred to many indigenous tribes. Speaking about them can be triggering, you may wish to skip this section.

One night two friends of Pablo found a dead owl on the road. They instinctively brought it to his house, Pablo looked at the owl's body and said it looked peaceful. Traditionally you don't bury birds as powerful as owls, you burn them to release them back into the air. Pablo used the term 'processed' to describe the transitioning into the next world for the owl. Pablo gathered certain plants and pieces of earth to prepare the ceremony. He turned to the man who had shown up with the owl, asked him who he's been thinking about recently, what happened in his mind when he picked up the dead owl, where are the people he loves now? These questions and their answers grounded the ceremony of processing the spirit of the owl as well as the traumas of the man. The man told Pablo about his losses, his struggles and that he had recently lost his father. Pablo removed one wing, its talons and tail feathers from the owl. The man noticed no blood had come from the owl as he cut each of the parts off. As the owl burned, he was asked to use the ceremony to process everything that the man had shared of his griefs, as the smoke rose above them, four other owls circled, hooting above their heads.

Both Jonny and Pablo had grown up in indigenous communities but with sensibilities a world apart. I on the other hand had grown up in concrete London, specially, in working-class Hackney in the 90s. An area, which, thanks to gentrification, has undergone a seemingly complete transformation. In the 80s it was one of the most impoverished and feared places in London, dramatised in British TV shows like *The Bill* and *Casualty* as a no-go area filled with 'Yardies' and Kurdish Mafia wars, but artists flocked to the area for the cheap rent and warehouses.

I was living (at different times) between my mother's house (which had one large tree in the back garden) and my father's Hackney council estate. Like Ellison, I identify as a City Boy, gritty clay from that man made earth – someone at home in the humming metropolis, the tall concrete staircases of tower blocks and skyscrapers. There is a rhythm to this living, a necessary tension that stops you ever lowering your guard.

In London, when I went for walks I turned my hearing aids off, in Oklahoma I started turning them up. The birdsongs, their range of sound would feed me something – some of the melodies were erratic and broken in intensity but I felt a slight bounce, a nourishing levity in what I would have once thought of as an overwhelm of sound. Oklahoma is vast, a striking landscape of lakes, grasslands, valleys, creeks and dramatic skies. The weather in Oklahoma knew how to stage drama, all of it fleeting, rain or shine, storm or tornado. One taxi driver put it well: 'If you don't like the weather in Oklahoma, just wait a minute', nothing is fixed, every season passes through rapidly, sometimes all of them inside one hour.

I saw two snowstorms and an ice tornado within my first few months there, experiences at once terrifying and beautiful. Both storms left the park by our house eerily silent and iced over. Some trees were so embedded in icicles they'd snapped in half. A patch of bright yellow flowers (coreopsises) that had recently bloomed had been iced in the Antarctic air, leaving the bright fire petals frozen in tubes of ice.

In the walks I took in the parks as the ice melted, I saw the birds returning to their trees and their songs. Near-silence came to gradual life. The sounds in this context were euphoric, the songs of birds that had survived and returned dizzy and chanting, a joyous lightness. This was my first real world encounter, (or at least the most striking) with the idea of birdsong and happiness. How it left me soulful, quietly charged, glowing in this sound show of nature.

In 1962, Ralph Ellison wrote an essay titled *On Bird, Bird Watching and Jazz*, exploring his favourite Jazz musician, Charlie Parker, who was nicknamed Bird. The lack of specificity intrigued Ellison; exactly what kind of bird is Charlie Parker? Ellison leans on his knowledge of bird sound and song, ruminating on the Yard Bird (Chickens) to Mocking Birds and Robins. How many of these sounds did Ellison first hear in Oklahoma? How subconsciously did Charlie Parker's sound root Ellison back in the land of his birth?

A year later I returned to the UK. I was commissioned to write a poem for a new building on the campus of Warwick University. The building is erected in the middle of forest-like terrain, contextualising the new department building as a kind of nest among the surrounding trees. Old and new knowledge can be incubated here. I spent a few days in the Warwickshire suburbs surrounding the city of Coventry. A city once rife with air raids. Tabitha had been offered a job in London so we knew we wouldn't be returning to Oklahoma. I was hit with an unexpected melancholy for the landscape that I was just beginning a relationship with – one that remains unresolved. The relationship, really, was with the birds and how they filled my days with brightness. In Coventry, there were birds, I kept my hearing aids up for them, but they were different. Their song was different. They had another context. Their songs announced a place that I am not a part of. They weren't city birds and perhaps I am no longer a city boy.

The poem I wrote while thinking and living through this time is called 'Resonance':

Resonance

The birds sound different in this city.
I'm new to their rhythms, can't place them easily.
Jarring, precise, I have to listen.

I've never been one for birds, nor envisioned
ever thinking birds were godly,
but the birds sound different in this city.

I bought audio books about birds – didn't listen.
Their names and looks uncharted astronomy.
But the birds sound different in this city.

They sing from trees in sleet storms, shy, persistent.
The birds sound different in this city.
The birds have invented a new religion.

Settling here was not my mission.
But wherever I live I live honestly.
The birds sound different in this city.

Walking these streets I feel forgiven.
The bells of the birds are auguries.
They tell me I've finally found a way of living.
The birds sound different in this city.

MONA ARSHI

Writing through a Pandemic

> patience, I think
> my species
>
> keep testing the shiny leave
>
> the spiny heart

JANE HIRSHFIELD, 'My Species'

The poet Louise Glück in 'Education of the Poet' writes that 'The fundamental experience of the writer is helplessness… most writers spend much of their time in various kinds of torment… it is a life dignified by yearning not made serene by sensations of achievement.'

Glück uses her words carefully: 'writer' not poet; a term that must be used cautiously in hushed tones. For that word contains something of the prophetic; the devotional; the paramouncy of the journey as opposed to the concern for the destination itself or maybe that's what I choose for it to mean

I write this from hibernation. The city of my birth, London, the UK, its economy, its humans have paused. We poets are used to such pauses in our strange enterprise, we reach them at breath points and line breaks or rhetorical emphasis. We are at home with caesura — in verse scansion a mark which looks like tram lines or perhaps more like a crossing, what's unclear in the image is the height of the two dividing walls and what lies within the narrow field between the two points. The mark also appears in the word *fallow*.

But if this current imposed pause feels familiar that's because it is to, me at least. Fifteen years ago, when I was a very different person, my work as a human rights lawyer was suspended. I was waiting to be a mother, pregnant with twins; an unstable pregnancy which necessitated being at home for almost three

179

months. Whenever people ask me how long I have been a writer I tell them that's easy, my writing age is the same age as my children.

This is when I re-encountered poetry, slowly and seriously. After a decade in the world of precise legal rules, I became fully immersed in the language and metaphor of the ephemeral, the quixotic, and the uncanny. I stepped into Romantic poetry, ghazals, and overdosed on the confessionals. I mothballed my lawyer robes and court suits and dived into a new life.

I was fortunate to come across the work of the poet Wisława Szymborska early on. I learned from reading her and many of the Eastern European poets that a poetic line is capable of bearing almost any human experience. 'Whatever inspiration is,' Szymborska said, 'it's born from a continuous "I don't know" and that genuine poets keep repeating "I don't know".' Most poets will tell you that this this uncertainty is the foundational principle of poem-making.

I've run out of the number of people who've asked me how much I can use this cessation as time to write. They mean it kindly. I usually have full mornings to read and write and feel ungrateful when I cannot. I have barely written two lines and even those I will probably cross out. Poems are wretched things to conjure at the best of times, but I've always thought though they bloomed in some otherly peripheral space they might still be delicately captured somehow. I have recently completed a novel whose protagonist Ruby is a selective mute, Ruby is a compulsive talker but only in her head and most of it angular and strange. I wrote in her voice for five years at the same time as writing my second book of poems, flitting from one pole to the other. When I think about that now I don't actually know how I managed both at the same time without pausing. Can you serve two mistresses? I don't know. Sometimes I felt like an adulteress conducting an elaborate secret affair.

Anne Carson famously said that 'If prose is a house, poetry is a man on fire running quite fast through it.' In my house the poems anguish in the attic and can only be reached by the fire escape ladder from the outside and the prose sits impishly taking up all the space on the living room sofa.

The writer Tillie Olsen died at the age of 94 in 2007 and her seminal volume *Silences* published in 1973 still contains some of the most important thinking around the battle most writers will have with the blank page and the obstacles in place for women and mothers who may fall into silence. It's a book I've often been in need of particularly when my children were young. She is less interested in the natural silences (Keats referred to these as *agonie ennuyeuse* – a term that saying aloud even sounds painful) the silences she speaks of are the other kind 'the unnatural thwarting of what struggles to come into being but cannot'. This made me interrogate what other reasons were preventing me picking up my pen. But even Olsen would have battled to get her head around the strange and gruelling dilemmas facing the writer in this modern pandemic.

*

It's true to say the present conditions make it difficult to concentrate. There's new white noise underneath everything. This anxiety-hum has shifted my concentration. This is no real hibernation. We have become hyper-vigilant animals. As a result, I can only read short and sharp-edged things. I am mainly reading the ancients, poetry and fables. I have also paused with my children: my teenagers. Untethered from schooling in any conventional sense they are sleeping the pandemic away. I often read them fables, the darker the better; they love the supernatural. They seem shocked when I tell them that in the original version of Rapunzel the Prince impregnated her early on in the story. There's something reassuring about the fact that our ancestors uttered these stories out loud like spells and they became instructions for living or outlining of some dharmic law. Not surprisingly reality gently seeps into our dreaming. Our family sleep like bears; we have such clear and fantastical dreams and when we wake, we collect them together at the breakfast table like roadkill and gently poke them. One evening I read the Virginia Woolf short story 'A Haunted House' about a ghost couple searching for something in their old beloved home there are lines such as *'Wandering through the house, opening the windows, whispering not to wake us, the ghostly couple seek their joy.'* The next morning there was a dead wasp near my pillow.

*

The English language and its culture are partial to metaphorical speech and our government leaders have deployed images of war and the Churchill war-drive as part of our government narrative to do battle with the 'enemy virus'. We are at war. Parks are closed. Police powers enhanced, I go for a state sanctioned walk a day and it feels less like a battle and more like submission. There are days I have to remind myself I used to be a human rights lawyer. Good citizens stay at home; bad ones go shopping for non-essentials and spit on the pavement.

All the while there are the numbers. 920 one day, 734 another. Friends lose fathers and grandparents, loved ones get ill and we exchange texts 'How bad is it?' I ask a friend. 'You really don't want to get this,' says my newly recovered friend, I can still hear the faint wheeze in her voice when she talks. Attending funerals is impossible so I've sent and uttered prayers and poems instead. Poem and prayers have always been close cousins of course. Prayers contain the scent of the familiar. There is an ancient logic that that familiarity activates. The literary critic Helen Gardner once said 'people don't want fresh insights from Hymns'. In a largely secular country, we cannot doubt poetry's deep participation in the ritual. The reality is that most poems are not cures or remedies or balms and they don't pretend to be, in fact they are very often the opposite irritating misbehaving miscreants. But prayer is often the last resort of the desperate , uttered for the dying and the dead, and poets (including myself) have used the form tirelessly.

I wonder if pausing sometimes is a necessary part of being a writer as essential as the writing itself, that we need these natural pauses to incubate a dream or inhabit an idea and feel free to turn over the stones in the garden. If you were to ask me one essential requirement for writing poetry (or as aspire to poetry as Glück talks about) I would say it was the close-listening that some people refer to as attention. This means in the ordinary sense of giving heed, an active direction of the mind upon some object or topic. We do literally have to arête – pause to attend to something closely.

When we do this something is stripped away. It's the poetry's distillation and abstraction that is so essential to the human that we recognise it immediately, the poet Paul Celan spoke of it 'as a sort of homecoming'.

You principle of song, what are you for?
DENISE RILEY, *from* 'A Part Song'

Eight years ago, my younger brother died suddenly. We all moved into my mother's house and cocooned ourselves in that space for a month. I pushed morsels of food into her mouth and said prayers and we waited for the pain to pass. When my brother died I had quite a big quarrel with poetry. I had only just started on my poetry journey and now I was confronted with this. Where was my mourning tongue when I needed it and how could language fail me so utterly? Eventually it was possible to write again, though so much of the first book I wrote feels like an attempt to write against this impossibility. I didn't know then that the depth-charge of grief detonated slowly. I spent most of the years following his death writing about it.

I recall Seamus Heaney saying the impulse that drove his poem 'Mycenae Lookout' (which centres on the enslaved Cassandra) written after the Irish peace settlement was begun as a 'snarl rather than a hymn… the way a construction worker starts with a pneumatic drill'. The lines of the poem are ferrying years of devastation and suffering in bare-boned tercets.

How does one write in the disaster or about one? Sometimes I think that it's not that language that is failing it's just that we are failing to understand what the language is asking of us and its okay to say, 'I don't know.'

When I last visit my mother, it's a still and warm April afternoon and we meet, socially distanced in her garden. For the first time in my life, I see and hear the green parrots puttering in the trees. I wish I knew the names of birds I notice and or could identify trees by their leaves. My parents have always lived under the Heathrow flightpath and now manage another first: a conversation in the garden uninterrupted by Boeings. I look up and there is not a single plane track scarring the sky. The odd feeling is that although we are living such local lives reduced to essentials, I have never felt more outwardly and compassionate towards the world. We discuss a photograph of Jalandhar in Punjab where my family live, and the Himachal chain of mountains is visible to the residents for the first time in over 30 years. The image is so serenely beautiful and the thought that my cousins might have this view now makes me weep. I want things to return to normality – I don't want things to return to normal. I remind myself that what I find in poetry and in nothing else in the world is the space to sit with uncertainty and doubt and ambiguity and the need for poetry is the need, as Mandelstam says, for us to be entwined 'in the bright-haired wave of its breathing'.

LEO BOIX

Multilingual Writing and Translation:
A Poetics of Resistance

The Maya Codices, written by the pre-Columbian Maya civili-
sation and destroyed mainly by conquistadors and Catholic
priests in the 16th century, abound with figures of scribes and
local poets with heads bowed to their writing tasks. Often
undeciphered glyphs float before their bent heads, symbolising
perhaps the mysterious transmissions that all poetries in transla-
tion augur. Some of these figures also locate the origins of Latin
American poetries in pre-Columbian writing systems. The figures
of the scribes and poets were taken from vases in the codex style,
a reminder of the Spanish conquerors who read diabolical intent
into the unfamiliar forms of Maya writing and set out to destroy
these sacred books, largely succeeding. Maya glyph writing is
considered by many as an indeterminate system designed to
encourage word play, but also a system that contains tendencies
but not absolute rules. It is a system of coding and decoding, of
rendering ideas from one source to another, in an endless circle
that continues even today with the work of contemporary poets
from indigenous communities of Latin America.

The quipu system, a recording device fashioned from strings
historically used by several cultures in the region of Andean
South America, could also be understood as a pre-Columbian
system of translations and mistranslations. The Inca people
used these knotted strings primarily to collect data and keep
records, monitor tax obligations, compile census records and
calendrical information, and for military organisations, among
other essential functions.

Scholars have challenged the traditional view that the quipu
was merely a memory aid device. Many suggest that it may
have progressed towards narrative records and became a viable
alternative to the written language just when the Inca Empire

collapsed. It allowed for a multilayered reading of the world, with multiple temporalities, histories and languages. They could also take the quipu with them, enabling the scribes to move from place to place, to take their stories wherever they went.

The Peruvian poet and artist Jorge Eduardo Eielson (1924-2006) explored some of these ambiguities and complexities in his work by writing profusely about quipus and its various meanings and making artwork inspired by these endless knots. He started producing quipus in 1963, some of which he showed in the Venice Biennale of that year. He continued to develop a distinct visual and verbal language of knots to convey a world of interconnected ideas, thoughts and illuminations. Some of his better-known poems are, in fact, types of verbal quipus. 'Knots/ That are not knots/And knots that are only/Knots' Eielson wrote in 2002 as part of his last collection, suitably titled 'Nudos' (Knots). In that book, he emphasised the idea of the knot as a conceptual bridge enabling the poetic language to expand and move in unexpected directions – knots not only as words, verses or even poems but as entire universes connecting different realities and emotions. 'Knots that say nothing/And knots that say everything.'

It is fascinating to note that these complex knowledge systems were rooted in Latin America and its people, allowing for vital connections between languages, cultures and historical specificities.

One can often see these systems as having much in common with multilingual writing and the process of translation/mistranslation, something I have been exploring in my work since becoming a bilingual poet and translator.

Writing poetry in both Spanish and English, experimenting with the ambiguities and political nuances of Spanglish, and translating poetry by contemporary poets from Latin America into English, has allowed me to look at multilingualism and translation differently.

It has let me explore the complexities of my own linguistic and cultural experiences as a writer and translator born and raised in Argentina, where Spanish and many indigenous languages such as Quechua, Aymara, Guaraní and Mapudungun (to name just a few) are spoken daily, but now living and working in the UK, a place where English is the dominant language.

In this respect, I relate to the experiences of many US Latinx writers who have thrived in bi- and multilingualism, incorporating English, Spanish and many of the indigenous languages of Central and South America and other emerging subaltern influences in their work.

It is precisely because of that multicultural and multilingual experience in the US and elsewhere where Latin Americans have emigrated (Spain, France or England could be an example) that poets and writers of the so-called border have rendered their experiences in a more nuanced and intersectional way.

According to Ed Morales in his seminal book *Latinx: The New Force in American Politics and Culture*, the mestizaje and multilingualism that emerges through Latinx mixed-race identity for several centuries 'is strongly grounded in bodies and spiritual tradition'.

For Morales, border thinking and border writing 'has always been present across the Americas, but as the twenty-first century unfolds, it is poised to take on a more prominent role'.

Here in the UK, we have already seen a new generation of Latinx writers exploring the idea of multilingualism and inter-sectionality in their work, taking it to a whole new level. The Scottish/Mexican poet Juana Adcock, the Peruvian/British writer Karina Lickorish Quinn, the Brazilian-British novelist and activist Yara Rodrigues Fowler and the Latinx poet Maia Elsner, born in London to Mexican and Polish Jewish parents, are just but a few examples of this exciting new generation of writers. They are all experimenting with multilingualism, exploring multiple linguistic and cultural identities in a multi-cultural and multiracial UK.

Editor and activist Nathalie Teitler, in her introduction to the anthology *Un Nuevo Sol: British Latinx Writers*, has rightly pointed out that all these writers have many common threads running through their work. From the experimental nature of their writing and playfulness around language (Spanish/English/Portuguese/Spanglish), to the use of coding/silence, focus on storytelling, rich imagery and the refusal to use Western tropes of linear time or a reality of only five senses. 'All of these things can be found in Latin American literature and make the voice of British Latinx writers one that both adds to the traditional British Canon and interrogates it,' Teitler adds.

For her, to be British Latinx 'is to live the experience of constantly translating yourself on all levels; to be accustomed to people addressing a version of you that bears little resemblance to your actual identity. It is to know what it means to be both present and invisible.'

All of this brings to mind a poem by Juana Adcock called 'On Love and Dying Languages', in which the poet explores all of these issues with incredible clarity and beauty:

> In our broken mother tongues,
> in our English plain,
> in our rented room,
> in our foreign country,
> with our migrant friends,
> little by little we built a vocabulary known only to us.

Like knots or Mayan glyphs, this new multilingual vocabulary rises against all odds to tell a new story.

> We developed our own syntax.
> The present continuous was always being lost.
> Articles were obviated.
> Dreams were something we saw, rather than had.
> There was no indirect object.
> The future was an act of purity of will.

Multilingualism is a tool to imagine a world with its syntax and multiplicities, one where past, present and future can intermingle, in which ambiguities are played out.

In his essay on Latinx culture and history, Morales states that the multilingual mind 'must draw analogies to process multiple meanings just as a multipositional consciousness works full-time to resolve the ambiguities of race'. For him, what Latinx can claim 'is the ability to imagine multiple others within one awareness, allowing otherness to fade as it becomes part of an internal conversation'.

In my debut English poetry collection *Ballad of a Happy Immigrant* (Chatto & Windus, 2021), I have looked at multilingualism as a new knowledge system drawing from personal, communal and collective experiences as a bilingual gay Latinx poet. I have experimented with Argentinian Spanish words within English verses in poems such as 'Godwanaland', 'Victoria Ocampo Writes About Meeting Virginia Woolf' and 'Autobiography in Three Columns', where language, syntax and cultural differences are turned upside down. I have also explored the idea of mistranslations in my collection, where I recreated or re-read Anglo-Saxon charms to create my own versions or readings of them. In both 'Charm for a Journey (A Mistranslation)' and 'Charm for a Swarm of Bees (A Mistranslation)' I have tried to subvert the idea of the perfect translation or the ideal rendering, by looking at what happens when words/meanings are lost in the process of translating from one culture to another. In both poems, I translated from Old English into my own English, creating a cultural version that responded to themes of diaspora, queer love and otherness. I have often wondered if we can fully render from one language to another and what gets lost in that process. Can we encompass these experiences, turning them into a 'vocabulary known only to us'? All these questions are intrinsic to the Latinx experience, especially when thinking of multilingualism, creative translations and mistranslations.

Furthermore, there is also the political implications in multilingual texts arising from the representations of linguistic plurality and encounter, the aesthetics and politics of linguistic border zones, contact zones, or translation zones.

Multilingualism can exist to challenge the national language, contest existing linguistic and cultural hierarchies (i.e. national language vs minority or immigrant languages), or complicate traditional, rigid categories of identity. Writing multilingually opens up new, more nuanced possibilities of literary representation and poetic thinking about human lives in their ever-changing social contexts, movement across and within different social spaces, or the always-existing mediation between selves and others.

It is a liberating process, a process of cultural and linguistic resistance, and a progressive paradigm that is as necessary as ever before in an increasingly interconnected 21st-century world.

JAY BERNARD

Manifesto: Stranger in the archives

1. The morning of the Grenfell fire, I picked up my phone and saw something about an incident in a building in West London. I thought nothing of it. I hadn't yet seen the photos, I assumed it was just another wave in the slurry of updates about other people's tragedies. Later, when I realised what had happened, I was immediately reminded of that other fire I'd been thinking about – New Cross, 1981. For the past year I have been reading and writing about that night, when thirteen West Indian kids died. As the scale of Grenfell became apparent, the similarities between the two emerged:

a) There is a mystery at the centre of both stories.
b) The people who died were not rich enough, in the eyes of the state, to be consequential.
c) The mystery is not how the fire started or why these people died.
d) The mystery is why we always find ourselves in the same place, the same moment.
e) A poet can't deliver justice but they can ask a different kind of question.

2. 'What does it mean when poets surrender vast realms of experience to journalists, to political scientists, economists? What does it mean when we allow the 'objectivity' of these disciplines to be the sole voice which speaks on events and topics of relevance to us all?' – David Mura

3. A few years ago, I decided to mentally tattoo a line by June Jordan on my left arm: 'I am not sure any longer that there is a difference between writing and living.' It has something of the aporia about it – it speaks to the unresolvable tension between

the time needed to write, the time needed to live. For many years I understood it as a kind of division of labour; while walking with an old lover, I saw it as the idea of writing something being the same as living it; during a recent panel at the British Library, Andrew McMillan responded to the quotation with something he says to his students – instead of theorising, go out and live; reliving is the latest interpretation to have materialised since I started working in the archives. I return to this line again and again to a) examine and practice June Jordan's hunch, which is also my own and b) make sense of my historical moment:

a) 'But a feminist life is also a going back, retrieving parts of ourselves we did not realise we had.' – Sara Ahmed

'Yet every working generation has to reclaim that freedom in time […] Capitalism is based on abridgement of that freedom.' – Adrienne Rich

b) After Grenfell, I knew that the media would immediately try to blame someone inside the house for the fire; that the first people to be arrested would be victims/minor players in the events; that there would be a fraught, exclusionary and botched meeting between the authorities and the community; that it would be down to the community to provide the support needed by the victims; that the tension, disgust and betrayal felt by residents and supporters would spill over into large-scale demonstrations, actions and possibly riots that the media would attempt to disconnect from the root problem of injustice. By writing about it, I can help shape history, contribute to the effort of keeping it alive.

4. What I have learned working in the archive #317: how quickly things are forgotten, how the act of archiving can be a way to forget; as the act of reporting something in the news can be a pacifier, a way to forget the initial grievance.

5. *Jubilee* – a reversal; when slaves are freed; debts are cleared; when all is reset and the cycle can begin again.

6. You can go from New Cross to Whitechapel, then switch to the Hammersmith and City Line, and then to Latimer Road station. As you pull in, you will see the tower's remains. For the first few days after the fire, thousands of people gathered to mourn, and I went down too. Everyone I knew was there, and we met each other in the street and stood in silence, or looked at each other, or tried to analyse the situation, but at bottom there was a strange electricity that always accompanies a gathering of people in the street. A strange sense of possibility, that the tower we were standing beneath was a physical manifestation of all that – all the things we said, all the things we felt, everything anyone has ever said, anything anyone has ever felt. The charred spine of a burned giant, jutting into the sky.

I am not sure any longer that it is possible to speak about myself without speaking about this.

7. 'It's queer black women who've developed and really curated a movement that is not about us. It is our vision that our movement is leaderful, decentralised, but we're not focusing our movement on our own ideologies or what we think is necessary and possible. What we do is centre why we think we should have all black lives mattering.' – Patrisse Cullors, co-founder of Black Lives Matter.

Standing below the tower, I realised the intensity of this statement. Queerness between the streets. Queerness not as relationship history or desire but as a stranger in the archives. Queerness as arc of history. Queerness informed by this tragi-carnival, this cycle of history. The work I have been doing on the New Cross Fire is the truest expression of queerness I have felt for some time: all-encompassing, outward-looking, rooted.

8. Backwards in time: to get from Grenfell to New Cross, you can take the Circle Line from Latimer Road to Baker Street, then Baker Street to Canada Water, then from there to New Cross via the Overground. Come out of the station, turn left towards Deptford and you will come across 439 New Cross Road. A tall, narrow house with a small front yard – smaller than you'd imagine. It is hard now to imagine the scale of the loss; not only the thirteen children who perished, but the faith,

the favourite dutch pot, the savings, the church dress, the diaries, the phone number written from one lover to another when they were still strangers. When I write about New Cross – about anything? – it's always about that.

Mudda she ah cry an she nah have no shoes
Man dem ah look but to help dem refuse
Fren dem shock by di scale ah di loss
Black smoke ah billow down there in New Cross

Me seh black smoke ah billow at di house in New Cross
Me seh black smoke ah billow at di house in New Cross
Me seh blood ah goh run for di pain of di loss
Me seh black smoke ah billow at di house in New Cross

MALIKA BOOKER

She Will Name Herself Ghost: She Will Haul Up a Poetic Courtroom and There Shall be a Reckoning

> The man raided like law was his warrant
> What right to raid the law like his warrant, his right
> The man persuaded/ raided/ marriage law his sanctity

'My Ghost in the Witness Stand'[1] is a work of reclamation and objection – as a site of resistance where a nameless protagonist resurrects and names herself, 'Ghost'. She who is never named in the telling of her gruesome tale in the King James Bible (KJV). She who is referred to as *wife, whore, concubine, unfaithful, unlawful wife, damsel* (emphasis mine), in Judges 19 (KJV), asserts herself as 'Ghost'.

Here, the 'Ghost in the Witness Stand' is a Caribbean woman, encumbered with legacies of the colonial project of plantocracy and the Middle Passage, defying the misogyny visited upon her body both in scriptures and in the Caribbean.

In that holy book (KJV), the abuse – enacted upon this woman's body through words (the very telling of the story of her gang rape) and actions (physical manhandling) are chilling. In Judges 19, we encounter 'one of the most sexually brutal and murderous texts in the entire Hebrew Bible' (Newsom, Ringe & Lapsley).[2]

The story begins with a wife who absconds to her father's house, and her husband journeying to retrieve her. Upon arrival, the husband is welcomed by the father then encouraged to drink and socialise. Each day his attempts to leave are stymied by the father-in-law, who encourages him to 'Be content, I pray thee,

---

[1] See p.130-33 of this book.
[2] The Women's Bible Commentary, third edition ed. Carol A. Newsom, Sharon H. Ringe & Jacqueline E. Lapsley (SPCK, 2014), p.123

and tarry all night, and let thine heart be merry' (Judges, 19. 6).

We are never told why the wife left her husband (the Levite) to return to her father's house. Yet according to Newsom, some Biblical scholars have used literary observations of the text to suppose that she was promiscuous. While others reject this translation as highly unlikely because a father would probably not welcome a sex worker back into his home. I am inclined to agree with feminist interpreters who 'surmise that perhaps the Levite abused her, and she could not stand the conditions of her life any longer and ran away' (Newsom, Ringe & Lapsley).

As a Black Caribbean female identifying poet, I have an ambivalent relationship with the KJV, enthralled by its lyricism, while critical of my positionality as a woman throughout the Old Testament in particular. Reading and interpreting the text from a female viewpoint has always felt as if this body is only a vessel for violence, shame, and judgement. While my black body is absent. My creolisation of the KJV enables women like 'Ghost' to liberate her voice and occupy centre stage.

Locating the female biblical body in the Caribbean enables an interrogative poetic vernacular that speaks to the legacies of the Middle Passage and plantocracy's impact on women's bodies.

> When one arrives in this world, in her body, our body, one has to make one's history in a way right, one has to make one's intellectual history, one has to make one's kind of erotic history, one has to make one's way in the world that doesn't record that history... [it is] an accounting that has to do with abstraction because the thing that is written is the record of the conqueror; there is another record. That is the record of the body.
>
> DIONNE BRAND, Tin House Podcast

And this is how it felt to me. There was my body attending church in Guyana on the East Coast Demerara, on Sundays in a small, whitewashed building, with the brown benches and magnificent pews, where a white priest commandeered our attention and even the pictures and statues decorating the church depicted whiteness. Images of a white Jesus, his disciples, and the Virgin Mary in her blue frock. There was no representation of my body or that of the predominately black congregation (decked out in their Sunday best) on any of the pervading iconography.

I was the staunchly rebellious little girl, disturbed by the punishments inflicted on women in the KJV for their transgressions, like Lot's wife being turned into a pillar of salt. Even at a young age I understood the significance of Lot's wife being rendered mute and the transient nature of her memorialisation. And this brutal treatment of the 'Ghost' in Judges exemplifies the extreme violence that has haunted me as both female and poet.

One of the main formal constraints of traditional sonnet is iambic pentameter (a stress metre), used to establish the rhythm of the voice as well as convey conventional speech. However, as Edward Kamau Brathwaite stated in a seminal lecture series[3] 'the hurricane does not roar in pentameters', nor can it capture the rhythm and flavour of the Caribbean. My sonnet sequence employs a Caribbean vernacular to enable 'my ghost in the witness stand' to embody and reframe the text by singing her own song, while responding to Brathwaite's challenge for Caribbean poets to lyrically capture 'a rhythm which approximates the natural experience…' (Brathwaite, p.10).

The history of the sonnet is one of patriarchal bias, from its origins with 'gendered roles of desiring, speaking male subject and desired, silent female object'[4] and a historical practice of establishing a tradition of sonneteers as predominately white western male. Even recent anthologies exclude women from the long history of sonnets with Edna St Vincent Millay and Elizabeth Barrett Browning being notable exceptions. If white women sonneteers are mostly absent from current anthologies, then black female sonneteers are non-existent. Yet there has been a long history of female/black sonneteers such as Marilyn Nelson, June Jordan, Rita Dove, Gwendolyn Brooks, Wanda Coleman, and Pamela Mordecai (to name a few) who have utilised and radicalised the form.

My poetry is concerned with legacies of colonialism and its impact on the Caribbean body by creating a subversive poetic that writes into silence and absence. From the 1940s Caribbean

---

[3] Edward Kamau Brathwaite, *History of the Voice: The Development of Nation Language in Anglophone Caribbean Poetry* (New Beacon Books, 1984).

[4] Jade Craddock, *Women Poets, Feminism and the Sonnet in the Twentieth and Twenty-first Centuries: An American Narrative* (PhD thesis, University of Birmingham, 2013), p.3.

women poets began to emerge onto the previously male dominated literary landscape. These women centred women's narratives and challenged the male occupancy of West Indian Literature. Una Marston, and later from the 1970s onwards, Lorna Goodison, Grace Nichols, Olive Senior and Merle Collins were all influenced by feminism, the Black Power and independence movements and began to craft embodied female narratives that challenged patriarchal male occupancy by giving voice to previously silenced women.

I aim to build on this tradition by enabling 'Ghost' to radically transform the androcentric sonnet form into a creolised song, address her absence in the KJV text as well as the impact and legacies of colonialism on her body. Here the shift between Caribbean and biblical landscape invites the reader to make correspondences between these two worlds, by illuminating the ways in which the KJV and colonialism help to shape attitudes to women's bodies and sexuality.

Using the sonnet lyric as a starting point and emboldened by different formal and structural constraints implicit in that form, the 'Ghost' transforms the sonnet sequence into a site of rebellion and a platform for free speech. As such, poetic constraints provide a vocal stage, enabling a counter-tale in which 'Ghost' recounts the reality of returning to and living with her father. Yet her telling is quite staggered, she halts, stutters, repeats and echoes.

> Like yard fowl I run   run back   to mi Poopa   yard
> but   but   he welcome   rancid as spoiled coconut
> water.   *What mek yuh run, come back, home, little gal?*
> over and   over like stuck record.

What does this repetition and echo represent? She ran back to her father's house. Not only does the nomenclature 'Father' connote biological father, but it also alludes to God. 'Ghost' radically opposes the patriarchal symbolism implicit in the text, by using the sequence sonnet as her platform to give voice to her circumstance.

>   When he   kick   kick
> our dog down concrete steps.   When crushed   hibiscus
> petals stained   stained our sheets   each morning's   bloom.
> But was not poppa's bosom a rock and hard   hard chest!
> His vile viper tongue hissed, *Sketel*,   hissed *salope*, said, *girl*
> *man have right to fling lash   in he wayward wife   ass*

The vernacular situates Ghost's body in Jamaica allowing her to address the patriarchy implicit in the region. The lines 'run   run back' also allude to marronage associated with runaways from the slave plantations to the bush – sites that can be read as either safe or unsafe, since maroons were known on occasions to make agreements with planters to hand runaways back.

Ghost's embodied voice and the sonnet form resonate beyond this historical reading and contextualisation. We notice the gaps, halts, and stuttering in each line of this re-telling. We notice the jagged rendering reinforced by white space. We notice how the layout of black on white evokes a staccato rhythm, a staggered musicality suggestive of her emotional hinterland.

> But was not poppa's bosom a rock and hard   hard chest!
> His vile viper tongue hissed, *Sketel*,   hissed *salope*, said, *girl*
> *man have right to fling lash   in he wayward wife   ass*
> finger pointed   pointed   to St James scripture, like   Judge
> verdict,   then fist   hammered wood. Yet I know in these

In *On Poetry* Glyn Maxwell states that 'poets work with two materials, one's black and one's white. Call them sound and silence, life and death, hot and cold, love and loss.'[5] Read in light of Maxwell's observation, the Ghost's fragmented utterance seeks to formally score their emotional terrain using the black and white material (victimhood and defiance and the tension in between) to address freedom and restriction.

Ghost's poetic monologue speaks to and about the father, whose grammatical translation to the Jamaicanised 'poopa', deepens his representation as her biological relative, but ruptures the ties to God the chief patriarch. The word, 'Poopa' allows the protagonists to sever links with the biblical patriarch – there is something soft and loving evoked with the arrangement of vowel and consonant. The way the mouth pouts to make the plosive p sound and hollows to form the o. That translation of father to Poopa creates a sense of the love the woman has for her father and makes the telling of his treatment of her chilling, while also implicating him in her subsequent death at the hands of her husband.

<hr>
[5] Glyn Maxwell, *On Poetry* (Oberon Books, 2012), p.90.

And on the fifth day, the Levite man finally objects to his father-in-law's delaying tactics and leaves with his wife, donkeys and servant. And as night falls, he sought refuge with an old man in Gibeah amongst the Benjamites. But when darkness came, the men in the city mobbed the house in a scene reminiscent of Lot's encounter with the Sodomites, (Genesis 19. 5-8) where they also demanded the visiting men (angels) be sent out to them that they may 'know' him.

Yet unlike Lot's story, where no one was sent out to the mob, the Levite pushes his wife / concubine (her label is interchangeable in these KJV scriptures) out of the door like a sacrificial offering, whereupon she is gang-raped all night by the mob.

Upon discovering her dead on the doorstep in the morning, the Levite takes her body home then proceeds to dissect her: 'he took a knife, and laid hold on his concubine, and divided her, together with her bones, into twelve pieces, and sent her into all the coasts of Israel.' (Judges 20. 29). Thus, rendering her dismembered body a catalyst, and sacrificial rallying call. And most importantly providing the inciting incident for the genocide, ethnic cleansing and rapes that ensue later in The Book of Judges. The Ghost uses the repetitive form of the Sonar Sonnet to counteract the biblical glossing over in the telling of the tale.

The formal structure for the witness stand is a sonnet with its inherent capacities for rhetoric and debate. The witness stand in this poetic courtroom seems an apt construct to interrogate language used in The Book of Judges.

My Ghost in the Witness Stand

*   *   *

A Levite persuades his unlawful wife to return to him – JUDGES 19

(Objection)

> · The man raided like law was his warrant
> · What right to raid the law like his warrant, his right
> · The man persuaded/ raided/ marriage law his sanctity

Persuades
    – Substitute dragged; hair clamped in palms
Persuades
    – Substitute with hand collaring throat
Persuades
    – Barricade breached, law unlawful to my body
Persuades
    – His right, his might, my flight – ask why?
Persuades
    – Picture fist hammering my cowering body, fake Tabanka smiles
Persuades
    – Picture his smiles at wife with grilled teeth
Persuades
    – Picture grip, and ignored, glass pressed into skin
Persuades
    – Picture body in a car trunk
Persuades
    – Picture body thrown, carted over donkey back
  Persuade
    – Picture punishable death.

The poem opens with the following quote from the Book of Judges (*A Levite persuades his unlawful wife to return to him* – Judges 19) and is followed by an objection on the part of the 'Ghost', who proceeds to provide a counterargument (all lines of the sonnet), before interrogating the verb 'persuades', suggesting that while 'persuades' in the biblical text alludes to the act of convincing, this was not so in the Ghost's case. She instead likens the interaction with her person to a raid, thus setting the stage for the subsequent cross examination of the term 'persuades'. There is a slight pun here as the sonnet is a rhetorical form, and according to the Oxford English Dictionary rhetoric is 'the art of effective or persuasive speaking or writing'. The structural form of the sonnet enables the setting up of a premise followed by a volta which could be a summary, a counter argument, a realisation. It is this aspect of the concluding sestet that allows the deconstruction of the word 'persuades' through an examination of its repercussions on her body.

The imaginative enactment of a lyrical courtroom enables a reckoning that begins with the bracketed (objection) signifying contention. The 'Ghost' uses the term substitute to replace 'persuades' with an experiential translation of the actions involved in her coercion. She is using a legal framework within a sonnet form in order to re-examine, deconstruct and decolonise the biblical narrative.

In *The Making of a Sonnet* Edward Hirsch notes that 'something about the spaciousness and brevity of the fourteen-line poem seems to suit the contours of rhetorical argument... The form becomes a medium for the poet to explore his or her capacity to bring together the heart, feeling and thought, the lyrical and the discursive. It is conducive to calculation and experiment – a closed form that keeps opening up.' [5]

Conversely in *The African American Sonnet – A Literary History*, Timo Müller argues that African American sonnets can be described as troubling spaces in American literary history. The authors conceived the sonnet as a space that can be occupied, reshaped, and expanded. They created sonnets that trouble the boundaries erected. According to Muller:

> Dove follows Wordsworth in conceiving the sonnet as a site of freedom and imprisonment at the same time. Yet whilst Dove retains the Wordsworthian notion of dangerous and liberating at the same time, Fred Moten welcomes disruption as the very source of political and aesthetic innovation. [6]

For me, the Sonnet is a poetic essay, a vehicle for debate and persuasion. It has been a political inhabitation of a radical activism in the African American landscape since the 1950s. Claude McKay (an American poet of Jamaican birth and parentage) used the sonnet to give voice to protest poems such as 'If we must die...' – a sonnet McKay claims was written for the 'abused, outraged, and murdered whether they were minorities or nations all over the world'. With these contingencies in mind, I queried how appropriate this constrained form would be for 'My Ghost in the Witness Stand'.

Karen McCarthy Woolf invented the coupling form in her collection *Seasonal Disturbances*. In an interview with Fiona Sampson for *Mslexia*, McCarthy Woolf explained how she came

[5] Edward Hirsch, *The Making of a Sonnet: A Norton Anthology*, ed. Edward Hirsch & Eavan Boland (W.W. Norton and Company, 2008).

[6] Timo Müller, *The African American Sonnet: A Literary History* (University Press of Mississippi, 2018).

across an excerpt on horse chestnuts from Thoreau's journals and started to lineate the prose paragraph on screen. As the coupling developed the aim was to think about a response line 'to integrate or extend the two voices, but also to subvert or extend what the original writer was saying.' I noticed that the form set out in couplets encouraged interruption, a connect and disconnect as the responding line also had to mirror the original line in some way. McCarthy Woolf asserts that 'the response line is intended to act as an asymmetric mirror of the original, you might use rhyme, assonance, repetition or a variation so you might have "memory" and "enamour", or play with the sound or meaning. It is a sonic quality that most favours the lyric.' I wondered what would result from merging a coupling with the Italian sonnet while retaining the debating character of the sonnet and conversational mode of the coupling? What emerged was a persuasive vehicle for the ghost allowing Ghost to address the biblical text and establish her own discourse. McCarthy Woolf has stated that the form can be 'interventionist, even revisionist' or 'act as a form of literary critique'. It offered me as poet and 'Ghost' a 'poetic device through which we can resist, interrogate, amend, and refresh the canon.'[7]

My writing has always explored the taboo and unspoken spaces that marginalised Caribbean women occupy in the political landscape. I have written and performed female centred monologues in theatre (giving voice to Windrush or fertility experiences). My last collection, *Pepper Seed* used autobiographical female narrative poems to speak to plantocracy's affects on my own Caribbean family and ancestors. A family geographically located in the Caribbean and diasporic spaces of Guyana, Grenada, Trinidad, Brixton and Brooklyn.

My poems are characterised by a Biblical and vernacular cadence, using narrative strategies like anaphora, and lamentation for musicality and effect. This biblical project stems from a desire to push further into canonical disruption employing formal strategies like the sonnet. I see the Italian sonnet as a lyrical essayist, a compact container that can hold a sophisticated argu-

---

[7] Karen McCarthy Woolf, 'Making a poem', interview with Fiona Sampson, *Mslexia*, Dec/Jan/Feb 1014/15, p.49.

ment, due to the turn (volta) which enables a thought/argument to pivot. While the coupling enables conversation, a call and response that is a necessary strategy for women asserting themselves into the KJV. The hybrid coupling sonnet form, also allows for discursive possibilities and enables embodied discussion between the women and the biblical text. This structural intervention is a necessary act for me as an intersectional feminist black womanist writer. It is the ability to use this hybrid form to empower the silenced woman voice that has consolidated the use of biblical and vernacular cadence in my poetics, heightening musicality and tension.

The courtroom sonnet is also informed by the decolonial work of female diasporic poets like m.nourbeSe Philip and Nicole Sealey, who use courtroom testimony to give voice to silenced narratives and deconstruct the impact of language on black and global majority bodies by situating their erased bodies in the witness testimonies. Yet while both writers evoke a fragmentary poetic, I have taken a more formal approach, choosing to create a lyrical courtroom sonnet in order to address and problematise the 'Ghost's' biblical narrative.

My poem 'My Ghost in the Witness Stand' could also be read as a tightly constrained textual performance, rooted in historical legacies of colonisation and miscegenation visited on the biblical and Caribbean woman's body. Here the poetic, although rooted in the sociohistorical, also enables the persona voice to stage a legal reasoning. The poem is therefore a podium for the airing of grievances, a pulpit for engendering disputes and disruptive in that it promotes a decoding of the word 'persuades' inspired by and in conversation with the poet Layli Long Soldier's interrogation of the term 'Whereas'.

Like Long Soldier's treatment of the word 'whereas', 'My Ghost in the Witness Stand' seeks to interrogate the term 'persuades', providing alternative definitions for her embodied experience of the word. Arguably it creates a lyrical spectacle and through the use of repetitive alliteration 'persuades / picture'. And most importantly the anaphoric repetition of 'persuades' (not unlike Long Soldier's repetition of *Whereas*), at the beginning of each line. A tactic designed to emphasise and build like a litany which is forcibly dismantled as the protagonist gradually unpicks the term 'persuades' line by line.

Ghost's 'reckoning' is neither confrontational not accusatory; it is not a 'writing back' it is an assertion of her own autonomy – a reclamation of her personhood/selfhood. My work has always strived to address the taboo. As I write in the wake of a pandemic where I watched the figures for femicide rise, across the Caribbean, read news reports of dismembered body parts being found scattered in numerous locations and watch protestors marching and Soca musicians speaking out about the need to take measures and raise awareness of the violence inflicted upon women's bodies, I am reminded of the relevance of this work.

RISHI DASTIDAR

Wanted: a screwball poetics
On why we should try to find comedy in poetry

> BURNS: It would have worked if you'd been satisfied with just being editor and reporter. But no! You had to marry me and spoil everything.
>
> HILDY *(indignantly)*: I wasn't satisfied! I suppose I proposed to you!
>
> BURNS: Well, you practically did! Making goo-goo eyes at me for two years till I broke down. And I still claim I was tight the night I proposed. If you'd been a gentleman you'd have forgotten all about it. But not you!
>
> HILDY *(speechless)*: You – you –
>
> *She grabs something and chucks it at him. He ducks. The phone rings.*
>
> BURNS *(to Hildy)*: You're losing your eye. You used to be able to pitch better than that.
>
> from *His Girl Friday*, dir. Howard Hawks (1940)

(0. Apologies for the lack of humour in what follows. Isn't that always the way when you're attempting to write about the comedic? Mirthless prose flows across the page with a gleeful ease.)

1. I have a weakness for the gag, the pun, the wisecrack, the remark that tries to be cutting, often fails, not least as it is delivered too late, or at the wrong time. I have tried to rationalise this away as I have got older, but frankly, I have failed.

2. My defence is two-fold: a) What is the hurry to grow up? and b) If you don't take the opportunities to make someone laugh – or laugh yourself – when you can, you get your comedy card taken away from you.

3. (NB: please note that I am not also claiming that *I* am funny – that is always someone else's judgement, and I wouldn't even want to begin to sway your views in that regard, one way or the other.)

4. So then: the main question is: where is the funny in most contemporary poetry?[1] After all, a punchline is to a joke as an epiphany is to a poem.[2]

5. You can go weeks, and read loads of poems and not get even so much as a slight upturn of the lips, let alone a titter, a guffaw, or anything more explosive.

6. Have you ever read a poem and done a belly laugh? Unlikely, right?

7. And I bet you're feeling a bit grubby right now thinking that that might even be a bit of a possibility.

8. I suspect you'll cop to loving this, by Nael aged 6:

> The tiger
> He destroyed his cage
> Yes
> YES
> The tiger is out

But not much more than that.

9. Which question begs: why is that? Are we suspicious of laughter as a reaction when reading a poem? Isn't that odd? Is it fair to say that poets, more than any other type of writer, are more suspicious of it as a reaction, let alone the possibility that

---

[1] I am taking it as read that we can agree that there are plenty of laughs to be found in English poetry from 'days of yore' (anachronistic phrasing very deliberate). Just off the top of my head: Donne's 'The Flea', Herrick when he's not being saucy, Stevie Smith et cetera.

[2] There is another parallel, as ventured by a copywriter friend of mine who once suggested that poetry readings were better thought of as failed standup comedy sets. Don Paterson has also talked about the fact that some poets (I absolutely include myself in this) are so desperate for any form of reaction from an audience that they try to engineer a laugh, whether it is there to be had or not.

it might be engineered as a desired reaction? Does it hinge around unspoken, unchallenged ideas of sincerity within the poem itself, and that any laughter, inadvertent or otherwise, destroys the spell the poem needs to cast?

10. Or put more directly, would people know that the poet is being sincere, and that they mean what they're saying, if laughter occurred as a result of the poem?

11. Isn't it odd to be suspicious of laughter as a reaction to certain types of art? I have been known to guffaw when standing in front of a Caravaggio. I accept this makes me odd – but is it an invalid reaction to the painting?

12. There must be a guilty party for this state of affairs.

13. *J'accuse* Pam Ayres!

14. I mean, she must be to blame, right? If she hadn't written things like 'He Never Leaves The Seat Up',[4] we'd all be a lot more trusting of humour in poetry.

(15. Except that she didn't write it.)[5]

16. She must be to blame. She's been called 'the nation's doyenne of doggerel'. Who amongst us will disagree?

17. But look at the rhetorical slight of hand I've just performed – implying heavily that 'funny' automatically equals 'doggerel'.

18. No other form writing that aims at being funny has to suffer that sort of calumny. No one disparages comic novels in the same way 'comic poetry'[6] is disparaged – it either is funny or it isn't.

---

[3] I could, I suppose, more substantively blame the 'art school turn' that contemporary poetry took in the 1950s, which brought it closer in theory and practice to conceptual art, where, as we all know, there are precious few giggles to be had.

[4] http://www.itakeyou.co.uk/wedding-ideas/wedding-readings-poems/he-never-leaves-the-seat-up.htm

[5] http://www.guardian.co.uk/books/booksblog/2012/aug/31/he-never-leaves-seat-up-pam-ayres

19. In a 2011 blog for the Poetry Archive Daljit Nagra said: 'Comic verse gets bad press because rigid notions of comedy foreground throwaway poems. Surely the best comedy is when the poem surprises us into laughter rather than setting up the expectation of laughter. The former leads to a complex self-evaluation whilst the latter leads to our judgement about whether the poet delivered the gag.' [7]

20. Which I agree with, apart from the underlying notion that you can't actively set out to make someone laugh.

21. What I am trying to say is that if a bad Martin Amis novel doesn't threaten the Western canon of literature, how on earth can a Pam Ayres poem that some readers of poetry don't like mean the whole notion of comedy in poetry is to be viewed as suspiciously as a fox checking out KFC?

22. I am aware that, as of yet, I haven't actually defined my terms – what is a comic voice in verse? Humour in poetry? Is this actually part of the problem, because what makes someone laugh is necessarily so subjective?

23. I mean, I think 'This Be The Verse' is not just deep and wise and true, but also mordantly funny. I suspect people don't want to acknowledge that last bit, because they fear that that might, in some way, diminish the power of Larkin's sentiments in the poem, make it in some way less deep or wise or true.

24. And of course, that's just nonsense. The humour is an integral part of it, and you can't get to the truth without considering the funny. The fool says.

25. Eye, beholder, you know the kind of thing. The following quote is long, but is pithier and smarter than this essay in its entirety so thank you Matthew Rohrer:

---

[6] Now that I've typed it, I'm not even sure it's a thing.

[7] Annoyingly, the Poetry Archive's blog, um, archive, has been deleted since this essay was drafted.

Why is John Ashbery considered a serious poet? His poems are often ridiculously funny and campy satires of all we hold sacred. Yet Helen Vendler says 'in short, he comes from Wordsworth, Keats, Tennyson, Stevens, Eliot; his poems are about love, or time, or age'. And Harold Bloom claims that 'Ashbery has been misunderstood because of his association with the 'New York School' of Kenneth Koch, Frank O'Hara and other comedians of the spirit.' There's a suspicious double standard applied to certain humorous poets who have, for mysterious reasons, been welcomed into or excluded from the canon of serious art. Ashbery's critics obviously find his idea of funny funnier than Frank O'Hara's funny or Ron Padgett's really funny funny. Padgett and O'Hara have written scores of poems about 'love, or time, or age', and some of them have been funny, and some have been serious, but they are written off as 'comedians of the spirit'.[8]

26. Of course, deep philosophical truths and humour can co-exist, perfectly comfortably, as I will now prove in the following Ph.D about screwball comedies... kidding.

27. No, a more fitting piece of evidence is the work of Wendy Cope.

28. (You didn't think a discussion of humour in poetry wasn't going to feature Wendy Cope did you?)[9]

29. I'll be unashamedly blunt and direct here, and damn the snobbish consequences. I think she's great, with a musicality and a directness of touch that means she hits her targets more often than not.

30. Here is 'Timekeeping', for example:

Late home for supper,
He mustn't seem drunk.
'The pob cluck,' he begins,
And knows he is sunk.

---

[8] https://poets.org/text/serious-art-thats-funny-humor-poetry

[9] I suppose I could have done the exercise with 'poet laureate of Twitter' Brian Bilston, but... no.

31. Now, of course, you could chose to throw the kitchen sink at the writing up of this bagatelle, and try to load it with pathos and bathos and angst and woe and despair and suffering, condemning the tyranny that the man is placing the woman under, the lack of empathy and understanding that she is displaying, while constructing a superstructure that bemoans and bewails the economic restrictions that traps them in their respective, reductive roles while providing the means of the immiseration in so handy a format, viz the presence of government-licensed drinking dens in local communities.

32. But I would wager nobody would read that more than once.

33. Because, as the best comedians will tell you, funny can be serious too.

34. See for example the oft-quoted, 'Comedy is tragedy plus time' said Carol Burnett.

(35.
> 'A funny poem is a joke with
> misguided ambitions
> and
> poor enjambment,'

said Rishi Dastidar, destined to be quoted by nobody.)

36. Of course, there is one type of humour that's allowed, and that's black humour.

37. There's nothing like a bit of *dark*, is there? We can all agree on that.

38. Especially as we're living through a moment where dark is cool, and dark is sexy.

39. Though we are due to move from dark to apocalyptic quite soon, and somehow, total annihilation and the end of the world seems more colourful to me; clearly I'm focusing on the process rather than the outcome, the black void at the end.

40. I would like to suggest you don't get better, blacker and funnier than:

> 'O Oysters,' said the Carpenter,
> 'You've had a pleasant run!
> Shall we be trotting home again?'
> But answer came there none –
> And this was scarcely odd, because
> They'd eaten every one.

41. I never did trust the Walrus. You probably shouldn't trust dogs either, or at least, well, be on your guard, especially when hunting: 'In Belgium, a man was shot by his dog / as they were just on their way hunting – a newspaper / carried the story under the rubric Funny Old World.' [10]

42. Here I should acknowledge that one of the few types of humorous poetry that is allowed exist without being looked down upon too much is 'Nonsense' verse, by your Carrolls, your Lears, your *Cautionary Tales* by Belloc.

43. 'He tried to prove a point in rhyme / My god that was a waste of time.'

44. Of course, that's different, as nonsense verse is only read by kids, isn't it?

45. And nobody trusts their opinions.

46. Oooh, I almost forgot! Satire! That's OK, that's allowed.

47. Satirical poetry. That's grown up. That's weighty. It has import.

48. Even *The Rape of the Lock*. Especially *The Rape of the Lock*. Pope is your default answer for the question, 'Name a satirical

---

[10] 'In Belgium A Man Was Shot By His Dog' by Durs Grünbein, translated by Michael Hofmann: https://www.poetryinternational.com/en/poets-poems/poems/poem/103-2237/auto/Durs-Grunbein/IN-BELGIUM-A-MAN-WAS-SHOT-BY-HIS-DOG?

British poet',[11] even though a pretty convincing case was made by David Hare in *South Downs* that, actually, as a representative of a pretty smug and self-satisfied elite who thought they were the acme of progress, he can't actually be thought of as a true satirist, as all he was doing was afflicting the comfortable without doing any of the comforting the afflicted.[12]

49. Best of all, you can stroke your chin and nod at satirical poetry, even if it isn't funny to you, because it deals with serious stuff.

50. I am being slightly unfair here, as some satirical poems can be savagely funny.

51. Like Michael Robbins' 'To the Drone Vaguely Realising Eastward', where the emphasis is on the savage:

> This is a poem for President Drone.
> It was written by a camel.
> Can I borrow your phone?
> This is for President Mark Hamill.
>
> Newtown sounds a red alert.
> Mark Hamill asks is Ernie burnt?
> Every camel's a first-person shooter.
> The Prez's fez is haute couture.
>
> It seems strange that he should be offended.
> The same orders are given by him.
> Paging Pakistan and Yemen.
> Calling all the drone-dead children.
>
> The camel can't come to the phone.
> This is for the drone-in-chief.
> Mumbai used to be Bombay.
> The bomb bay opens with a queef.[13]

---

[11] I think we can add Sam Riviere now too, and I was going to say McGonagall, but no one wants their name yoked with his do they?

[12] We should also acknowledge that there are plenty of problems with satire in of itself, as a practice, and for the fact that it basically doesn't change anything, as it can be so easily co-opted by the elites it is purporting to discomfort. For more on this see: https://www.lrb.co.uk/the-paper/v35/n14/jonathan-coe/sinking-giggling-into-the-sea

52. (By the way, 'queef' is a rude word? Who knew? I suggest we all give up this waiting for inspiration lark, and just write sestinas based on supposed insults we find in an Urban Dictionary.)

53. 'Queef' in its way points us to another dimension, that of satire working only because it demonstrates the flimsy line between reality and the whimsical and/or absurd.

54. If poems cannot traffic in the whimsical or the absurd – the funny peculiar, as it were – well we might as well give up. 'The best metaphors are always absurd when first chanced upon.' Discuss.

55. The unlikely often looks funny, at first, second glance, and every look after that.

56. Let us not wait for logic to reveal itself. Let us force logic to appear, by means of reconciling whimsical absurdities in such a way that we see anew, and laugh at this epiphanic revelation.[14]

57. What this does allow for is social comedy to reveal itself. Where perfectly normal interactions are destabilised, rendered strange, and so funny.

58. Such as in Joe Dunthorne's 'I decided to stop therapy':

> because I was perfect
> And how might your perfection
> appear to others?
> Classic my therapist,
> missing the point completely.

59. Or Holly Hopkins' 'Explanation for Those Who Don't Know Love', which if you are voluntarily childless will have you nodding if not howling in a glee of recognition: 'I have a child and am more important / than childless people.'

---

[13] Though I would be dissembling if I did not recognise that part of why it was so funny was reading the story behind why Yahoo! decided not to publish it, which you can find at: https://lareviewofbooks.org/article/a-poem-for-president-drone/

[14] Yes, that is a grandiose way to say 'punchline', what of it?

60. I should also mention: wit never used to be so looked down upon.

61. Yes, I know I haven't up until this point used 'wit' as a synonym for 'funny' or 'humour', but 'humour' me, here please.

62. (Clever wording, cheers.)

63. For proof of this download the 1996 film *Ridicule*, which shows how your status at the court in Versailles in the 18th century depended on your ability to throw out witty insults while avoiding them yourself.

64. When was the last time you saw an English-language film that was about language? Exactly.

65. I use the word 'wit' to also point out that it's rare to see poets described as 'witty'. I suspect most would dislike being labelled as such. It sounds insubstantial. Insincere.

66. And, dare I say it, some poets might prefer to be thought of as bland rather than insincere.

67. I should start trying to find some sort of conclusion here, for I fear this particular joke has dragged on too long. And I should try and suggest what a 'screwball poetics' might actually be.

68. I rather like this quote as a jumping off point: 'screwball comedies celebrate hard and chaotic love rather than security and the suburban dream. They favor movement over status and speech and argument over silent compliance.'[15]

69. We could take 'hard and chaotic love' as situations where black absurdity and unlikely scenarios fuse into a moment of joy. Come in Selima Hill: 'I want to be a cow / and not my mother's daughter. / I want to be a cow / and not in love with you.'

---

[15] http://www.yorku.ca/mlc/4319/03-04/gharavi/gharavi2.html

70. And 'movement' to me also speaks to playfulness as an idea, a mode, a spirit in which you could choose to read and write.

71. Because, I hope, it's fairly self-evident that play and funny are, if not bedfellows, at least knee-tremblers-in-an-alley-fellows. 'The play ethic,' says Pat Kane, 'is about having the confidence to be spontaneous, creative and empathetic across every area of you life – in relationships, in the community, in your cultural life, as well as paid employment. It's about placing yourself, your passions and enthusiasms at the centre of your world.' [16]

72. Funny and play and chaotic love – every screwball comedy ever, basically – takes us to joy. Not the quiet stuff, the laugh out loud, light up a room, yodel hosannas stuff. Oh hai Frank O'Hara:

> 'Oh! kangaroos, sequins, chocolate sodas!
> You really are beautiful! Pearls,
> harmonicas, jujubes, aspirins! all
> the stuff they've always talked about
>
> still makes a poem a surprise!
> These things are with us every day
> even on beachheads and biers. They
> do have meaning. They're strong as rocks.'

73. So: be more Burns, be more Hildy. Look for the zinger, the comeback in the stanza. Embrace the chaos, the argument, the zig and zag and ratatat of repartee, the bon mots of beauty and bathos. They are the stuff of poetry too.

---

[16] http://www.theplayethic.com/what-is-the-play-ethic.html

WILL HARRIS

Bad Dreams

I used to be obsessed with the question of what was real. I knew there were distinctions: the Hulk probably wasn't real – ditto the Power Rangers – but I couldn't rule out being able to fly or breathe underwater. These were real possibilities, as was the possibility – talked about in the summer of Year 5 – that two goo alien toys could make a baby goo alien. Reality could be freely altered or made anew. And this freedom, if it existed, was collective.

Back then, friends (and enemies) shaped the known boundaries of my world. One girl in class told me a story – stolen from *Goosebumps* – about an uncle who takes a scalpel to his nephew's brain to conduct a cloning experiment on him while he's asleep. That night I could see my uncle hunched by the door, waiting for me. But I wouldn't let myself call for help. I forced myself to remain silent, to be uncertain and scared until I was too tired to keep my eyes open.

Years later, in English, we read Sylvia Plath's poem 'Elm' in which an elm tree speaks back to the poet: 'How your bad dreams possess and endow me.' There was something sad and terrifying about that line; maybe it was the horror of being possessed by others' dreams, or the way Plath had extended the circle of possession (in all its senses) so that, suddenly, I couldn't look at a tree without seeing my own bad dreams staring at me. Dreams went out into the world. They gave a person or object qualities they didn't have, leaving them transformed.

Around that time, I'd sit for hours in bookshops on Charing Cross Road. One thing I wrote down in my notebook (by Camus, probably misremembered) became a sort of mantra: 'The natural is always acquired.' I copied it out into a word doc on my laptop; I carried it around in my head. It was a pre-emptive defence against accusations of unnaturalness.

Acquire feels part of the same family of verbs as *possess* and *endow*, all Latinate and connected to the transfer of wealth and property. My parents weren't wealthy. They left school early and, though they were both born in different places, they came to London with very little. They had no connections, no established links. Everything, for them, was slowly and painstakingly acquired.

I understood on a bodily level what it meant to acquire naturalness too. Sometimes people in bookshops were surprised that I could speak English or that I liked poems. My physical features were endowed with qualities from someone else's dream. In *The Day the Earth Stood Still*, the extraterrestrial Klaatu (played by Keanu Reeves) says: 'this body will take some getting used to. It feels unreal to me. Alien.' It was like that. I couldn't get used to my body, to how I was seen. When I entered a room I had to adapt to the expectations of others and acquire a naturalness that felt unnatural to me.

But in my mid-teens I started writing, building a shell around myself – like a goo alien – to block out the dreams of others. Writing was the least natural activity of all. It was hard. Every word I wrote only emphasised the gap between what I wanted to say and what I couldn't. I was writing poems having tripped into them, imitating the rhythms of things I'd read. It was the rhythm, the focus on sound, which temporarily removed the fear of failure. Because failure didn't matter in the same way in a poem. Poetry was already trying to do something impossible: to reach a place where words don't go. It was the music of language failing.

Throughout all this, there was the problem of race. Even before I could talk about it I knew what race was. It was the feeling of being possessed by other people's dreams. It was being defined by categories seen as natural rather than acquired. And maybe, I decided, poetry was the means by which to evade the possessive force of race.

With poems, reality could be freely altered or made anew. It was a form of collective making, affected and shaped by encounters with the world. When I came home to write, filled with the sounds of people and poems, the world was still with me; I was alone and not alone. I'd stay up all night. Poems were like bad dreams. I couldn't know what was real. But I let myself be uncertain and scared. I looked and looked at them until I was too tired to keep my eyes open.

NICK MAKOHA

The Black Metic

For a large part of my life, I have felt displaced. Removed from the centre of society by virtue of my social identity: a Black-African-Ugandan-Immigrant. I belong to multiple social groups that do not represent the centre of modern society, or more specifically whiteness. I am, therefore, living in a society where the media, literature, world news etc. demand that I perceive myself through the prism of the White gaze. To the British way of being (or the West/ First World), I am a hyphenated creature who is often perceived in derogatory ways. Inferior, a threat or a burden. These are bluntly drawn caricatures, with little connection to my actual lived experience, or identity. People have a tendency to see the world from where they stand. We are the sum of the stories we tell ourselves. What I have told myself is that I am in exile, that I am a man without a country, that I am a man who has lost his language, that I am a man always in between countries. My forced exodus birthed the poet in me. Georg W.F. Hegel's *Standpoint Theory*[1] states that where we place ourself in society in relation to the world around us is our standpoint. It also suggests that those with greater power in society see the world within a very rigid framework, whereas those with less power, view the world with more fluidity and nuance. In other words, being 'othered' impacts on the perception of reality and the lived experience. This feeling of being alien to the homeland I have left behind and also my adopted fatherland is not unique to me. It is an experience shared by an increasing number of people in the world. It is an experience that I came to realise has defined my identity & made me who I am: a Black Metic.

---

[1] L.E. Bailey, 'Standpoint Theory', *Encyclopedia of Queer Studies in Education* (Leiden, The Netherlands: Brill, 2021), pp. 676–82.

I originally wrote The Metic manifesto in the Spring of 2017 as part of my MA thesis. It was a term I developed to help me navigate my crisis of identity while developing my first poetry collection, *Kingdom of Gravity* (Peepal Tree Press, 2017). A Metic lens allows for a new precision in defining my identity. As a Ugandan poet/playwright living in exile I am a writer caught between two cultures. A Black Metic. This is a term I coined to explain the phenomena experienced by black poets in the UK. Metics are foreigners, or resident aliens whose allegiances are split between their homeland and their new country. Notable metics in history are Aristotle, Alexander the Great and T.S. Eliot. They have a different lived existence, an understanding that is forced upon them. An understanding of being that is both liberating and isolating at the same time, brought about through a unique experience of time and the way one moves through it. Metics express some form of liminality, an ambiguous position in cultural space betwixt and between the positions assigned and arrayed by law, custom, convention, and ceremony.

I came across the word Metic at the T.S. Eliot summer school. It was there that W.H. Auden's niece kindly introduced me as a shy young poet to T.S. Eliot's wife, Valerie Eliot. My feeling of otherness quickly disappeared as I dived into the workshops. All students and academics were connected by the language and poetry of Eliot. The characters in some of his poems are forced to deal with the question 'how do I fit in?' A question that intrigued me, particularly coming from a literary icon like T.S. Eliot. His work, *The Waste Land*, in its complex examination of post-war disillusionment, is often considered the most influential poetic work of the 20th century. For his vast influence in poetry, criticism and drama, T.S. Eliot received the Nobel Prize in Literature in 1948. His experiments in diction, style and versification revitalised English poetry, and in a series of critical essays he shattered old orthodoxies and erected new ones.

At one of the T.S. Eliot summer school talks a professor identified Eliot as a Metic. Being a native Bostonian in England, T.S. Eliot is contemporary poetry's most celebrated Metic. He was born in Boston and moved to England in 1914, at the age of 25. He became a naturalised as a British citizen, renouncing his American citizenship. His poems are the bedrock of British poetry and he is celebrated as one of the finest examples of the English canon. Matthew Hart charts for us Eliot's metic experience in his paper 'Visible Poet: T.S. Eliot and Modernist Studies'.

Hart points out [2]

> Eliot was aware of being a metic and expresses this is in a letter to his brother Henry in 1919:
>
> 'Don't think that I find it easy to live over here. It is damned hard work to live with a foreign nation and cope with them – one is always coming up against differences of feeling that make one humiliated and lonely.'

After the summer school I wanted to investigate the experience of Black Metic poets as a way of developing my writing process. I fled Uganda in 1979 with my mother, during the crumbling Idi Amin dictatorship. Terming myself a Black Metic allowed me to start formulating ways of writing about Uganda. I wanted to avoid being imitative and predictable. I wanted to speak with urgency and grace about difficult things. It helped me deal with my shame. I had to get over my resistance to looking at my origins in Uganda and dealing with the trauma of fleeing. I had to find a way to give myself permission to look into my past, to feel comfortable with my story. Indeed, a story is how we group the pattern of living, the explanation of life through personal and emotional truth, and a vehicle to search reality.

When I attended the Complete Works programme the number of Black poets published by major presses in the UK was extremely low (estimated at less than 1%). Black poets were often automatically labelled as 'spoken word', or 'urban' poets, irrespective of their actual poetry. In fact, it is fair to say, there are very few real conversations about craft in the writing of Black poets within the establishment. How does a young, emerging poet write into that space? A space that is, at best, an emptiness. An absence of understanding. At worst, a tangled mess of misunderstanding and stereotypes. These were the questions the first cohort of the Complete Works poetry faced. As the first cohort, we had everything to prove and little to draw on.

---

[2] Matthew Hart, 'Visible Poet: T.S. Eliot and Modernist Studies', *American Literary History*, 19 No. 1 (Spring 2007).

I wrote the Metic manifesto to clarify for myself, and for future poets, what I wanted my poetry to be as a realm of possibility. I wanted it to speak to the displaced writer of multiple geographies or identities. I think it began conversations in my mind about creating spaces for Black poetry that continue to guide me to this day. Its thinking underpins the purpose of the Obsidian Foundation retreat for Black poets that I later founded, modelled on the US institution Cave Canem.[3]

The Metic manifesto I wrote was published in the *Cambridge Review* as the 'The Metic Experience' on 6 December 2018. The plan was to develop the Metic manifesto further as a way of offering the black artist access to artistic freedom. The question most writers ask me is what exactly is a Metic? The term means a foreigner or resident alien whose allegiances are split between their homeland and their new country. The word itself – 'Metic' comes from the word *metá*, indicating change, and *oîkos*, 'dwelling'. In the ancient Greek city-state metics held a lower position in society. Being a citizen was a matter of inheritance. Metics did not become citizens unless the city chose to bestow citizenship on them as a gift, which rarely happened. Their political role was revoked. Metic is a Greek word which we might usefully read as a cognate of today's bureaucratic term 'resident alien'. But once we have got past the understanding of the metic, what next? A fish does not know it's a fish until it steps out of the water. I am not trying to prove to you that you are a fish. I am more interested in what type of fish you are. The ocean is not just a bucket full of salmon. If the ocean is literature and the fish is the poet, how can we identify your unique Metic experience? Furthermore, what agency does that give us in our writing?

I have been investigating how writers in exile are differentiated from natives, which I am using to explain the phenomena experienced by black writers in the UK and the US. The poets interviewed included seven African Americans (Chris Abani, Elizabeth Alexander, Gregory Parldo, Danez Smith, Nate Marshall, Rita Dove, Terrance Hayes) and four Black British poets (Kei Miller, Kayo Chingonyi, Malika Booker and Anthony Joseph).

---

[3] https://obsidianfoundation.co.uk

Metic writers are often homogenised in their experience, a homogeneity not allowed to be expressed in canonical tradition. Chris Abani distils this further when he says

> When you are a black person here, you are never an individual; you are always a collective. Whiteness enjoys that idea of being an individual. And so, whatever people have decided what the collective of blackness is, that is what you are until proven otherwise.[4]

The above writers are excellent examples of Black Metics. They are part of a new breed. The term encompasses them more than modernism, postmodernism, colonialism and post-colonialism. The historical terms act as forms of erasure. The term I hope counters this erasure. A Metic must negotiate the nuances of their story that consist of points of departure, return and initiation. At these thresholds of liminality there is an artistic opportunity to break through the myth of national identity. It is here that we can begin to recognise the Metic self that consists of the layered perceptions, multilevel systems and patterns of society, customary duties, and relational and familial positions. Each of us must seek to find our own Metic signature.

There are several observations to being a Metic:

1. Being a Metic is both liberating and isolating at the same time.
2. This liminality is brought about through one's experience of time and the way one moves through it.
3. Metic writers often find that when sharing their work they are homogenised in their experience.
4. Time, particularly the dimension of the present moment, is important to the Metic.
5. Metics often speak of a transplanted homeland.
6. Metics write to capture what they have come out of and there is a strong sense of place
7. The Metic uses art, as art endures its landscape and works against experiencing a sense of erasure.

---

[4] Chris Abani: 'The middle-class view of Africa is a problem', interview with Hope Wabuke, *The Guardian*, 27 July 2016.

8. Note that the Metic is not the alien; it is the area that he is transported to that exhibits the conditions of alienation.

What I am most interested in is the precision of identity that a Metic lens allows for. There are times when I want to be identified as an African writer, other times I would prefer Ugandan, other times Black-British, and other times I would like my life path to be represented: Ugandan-born, but raised in England, Saudi Arabia and Kenya. Writers of colour often feel pigeon-holed, needing to claim a single identity and remain married to it. Being a Metic means being a plural being, rather than a singular one. It pushes back against homogeneity. This manifesto is intended as a call to arms to claim the multitudes of our identities so that stereotypes about what we write will cease to inhibit our writing and our readership. My hope is that it will give other metic writers a lens through which to understand their complex identity, and to write it.

MOMTAZA MEHRI

An Emptying, A Gathering

Poetry necessitates solitude. This discipline of silence grounds a poet in the fertile soil of the imagination, batting away the cacophony of external distractions. Solitude has the effect of loosening, unshackling us from self-preserving pretence. We are all alone, and therefore, have no one to face, no one to answer to, but ourselves. James Baldwin wrote of the essential solitude of the artist, a cultivated 'aloneness' which could be best likened to the aloneness of birth or death. To him, it was the artist's responsibility to puncture society's delusional attempts to avoid the inescapable truth of this aloneness.

Life undermines any kind of cocoon. We know it isn't possible, or even justifiable, to seal ourselves off from the world. Refined disengagement is hardly an option. But without renewing quietude, the poet is left to the mercy of discursive chaos. You can't silence the outside world, but you can turn the dial down a little to better welcome the incomprehension of your own mind. Solitude rewards. It pricks and jolts, unravelling the fixity of easy assurances and claims. It demands much of the poet, including a barefaced openness to being unsettled. The presumptions we take comfort in, the ideological traps we make homes out of, the tried-and-tested narratives we prop ourselves up with; all fall away in the loneliest hours, dissipating under the grave light of solitude. We are left with ourselves and the reality of who we are, not who we want to be seen as. Uncertainty is the chink in the armour of self-conceit. A poetry of certitude is an inert poetics, a dull-eyed dead end. It only serves the tedious task of confirmation, congratulating itself and its readers on what they already know and agree upon. Above all, it celebrates the myth of a shared, foregone innocence. Such a poetics rejects, subtly and unsubtly, a confrontation with the world's gnarled misalignments, misarrangements, and misshapes. Solitude provides an environment for these inevitable confrontations, the unsteadying of the hand and the self. In stillness, ego-sustaining fantasies of permanence and purity are denied the room to thrive and grow. We need solitude more than we think.

I deeply believe in this restorative aloneness, and relate most to poets who crave it. Through it, I have furiously dug through layers of literary ventriloquism to find my own poetic voice. Yet, I don't mean to invoke images of the starving poet shivering in a garret, deranged by the weight of their unfulfilled talent. A call towards solitude isn't a championing of retreat, political quietism, or the singularity of artistic genius. It isn't a byword for inaction. I say this because at times, when I've felt the need to pull away most urgently – for the sake of my writing if not for myself – I've often felt strangely guilty. Even self-indulgent. Asked in an interview about 'the future of British verse', the poet Keston Sutherland differentiated between 'anxious and conservatively' narcissistic poets and 'radically narcissistic' poets. I've been thinking about this demarcation for a long time. Radical narcissism, as I see it, is a recognition of both the capaciousness and the limits of the individual. It's what can happen when we embrace the permeability of selfhood, allowing it to tear through us and our poetry, and then collectivising this transformation by sharing those poems. It's the recognition that such transformations are not ours to hoard, and that a poem is a way of thinking and doing that can lead to a changed way of being. Writing is a form of spillage. The poet is a magpie, but the magpie collects and collates in the service of nest-making, a project that sustains the lives of other organisms. I choose to believe in poetry's nest-making capacity. On and off the page, the poem is an arena for play, interrogation, friction, and fragmentation. When I turn to solitude, it's a way of shunning creative orthodoxies and the imaginative constraints they impose. I don't want to think about the 'poetry market'. I don't want to write a product designed to soothe and assuage. I want my poetry to ask useful questions. I want to be of use.

Solitude clears away the wreckage of identity. Black woman, African, diasporic, child of refugees, inner-city witness, worker, activist; as someone who has various labels thrust upon them and their writing, I know what it means to be an abstraction. Even the noise of well-meaning applause has the habit of drowning out individuality. Poetry offers us the gift of negation. It has taught me to approach my own life askew, and that I don't need to be comforted by labels or disguises. The margins shouldn't have to perform for the centre. The margins contain their own teeming, conflicted ecosystems, where influence is a slippery trickster that knows no borders. 'Stay loose,' advised Jack Spicer in one of his California lectures. 'Stay absolutely loose.' I share in his casual disdain for categorical enclosures, especially those that feel most natural to us. Our positions are as motile as our poetries. We should be willing and able to move between page and stage, between styles, traditions, tendencies, generations, coteries, and cliques. Or, to invoke Malika Booker, we can claim our 'right to be everywhere'.

But, amidst pockets of solitude, what becomes of poetic community? In the winter of 2016, I sent my application off to The Complete Works, having long admired the poets who had participated in the programme's earlier cycles. Deep in the throes of a 'lost decade' and a Conservative government's continued decimation of the arts, I was looking for a serious writerly community in an increasingly arid environment. Unsure as to what I was flinging myself into, I put off the deadline until the end, submitting at the very last minute. At the time, I didn't even call myself a poet. To me, it was a title others bestowed upon you. All I knew was that I had a blistering desire to share poetry with its practitioners and a need for a space to do so. I didn't expect to make the cut as a Complete Works Fellow, and when I was shortlisted, it was like a door had been pried open. I was finally accepted, joining the third cohort of poets. What followed was a meaningful broadening of the mind and the exhilaration of being read and taken seriously. Before The Complete Works, I had no model for a poet's life. I was quickly exposed to poets who had committed their lives to poetry and understood what it demanded of them. The Complete Works was one of those rare things: a creative development programme that wasn't interested in manoeuvres of professionalisation and optimised personal branding. Workshops, readings, retreats, discussions, disagreements, camaraderies; all served to sharpen our impulses and capabilities as poets and people. I was encouraged to think expansively, ambidextrously. While solitude has been affirming, I learnt that it was not, and shouldn't be, the only path. The kernels of that realisation began within the fold of The Complete Works, alongside many of the poets featured in this anthology.

By now, the impact of The Complete Works on the wider landscape of British poetry is undeniable. Notably, Bernardine Evaristo's efforts in initiating the 2005 *Free Verse* report, the first-ever survey examining opportunities for Black and Asian poets in the UK, laid the foundations for The Complete Works. The report's findings were dismal: only 1% of the poetry published by major UK presses was written by black and Asian poets. This statistic opens the preface of the first TCW anthology, *Ten: The New Wave*, highlighting the daunting literary terrain faced by minoritised writers, as well the tenacity of their vision. By 2016, and in no small part bolstered by The Complete Works, that figure had significantly increased by almost tenfold. Complete Works Fellows have won major prizes and residencies, shaping the direction of contemporary poetry and national conversations. Beyond the statistics, The Complete Works has been a galvanising force, asserting the vitality and resourcefulness of the poetry collective. It brought me in from the cold, showing me that I had something to give. Solitude and communality needn't be poles apart. The Complete Works nurtured its Fellows, granting us a space to tussle in the mud, crafting our own poetics, but always alongside each other, in a journey that is continuing and far-reaching.

KAREN McCARTHY WOOLF

It is lovely when... Diaspora poetics & the *zuihitsu*

It is lovely when a fragment can be a whole.

KIMIKO HAHN

*

A *zuihitsu* is a Japanese form that translates literally to 'running brush': generous in its relationship to disrupted thought, it holds together with a through line that could be geographic, thematic and quotidian—

*

Outside it's evening, there's birdsong, a cool westerly, chilly for May, even in London. My long-sleeved top's still damp, there's not been enough sun yet.

*

——its lexicon is the journal, the diary (picture a little lock clasped over an embossed cover, a key on a satin cushion...) which reaches back to its heritage text, Sei Shonagon's *The Pillow Book*—a 9/10th Century classic by a woman, written in colloquial (if courtly) Japanese, not classical Chinese as was usual for literary works of the time.

*

Lately, everything I write has a funeral in it, although I'm resisting now, because I've written many elegies and I don't want to be defined by my relationship to death (although ultimately, who isn't?).

*

Outside it's afternoon, in the cafe garden, slightly warmer, with a large seated Buddha and fire pit that sits next to the bell tower of a now re-purposed (residential, apartments) Swedish church, a crow is dive-bombing a squirrel on the corner of a roof. The crow sees the squirrel off and flies up to perch on an oxidised cockerel fixed to the steeple.

*

The *zuihitsu* operates via juxtaposition: a little clang clang between ideas, or moments, or items on a list.

*

Last week I went to my friend Jemima's mum's funeral and the wake was in the garden of a large Georgian house by the River Thames, and a funeral is a significant thing, a global ritual that all cultures share, so I've decided to mention it, which means I can now breathe out.

*

A long time ago, once upon, I attended a workshop with Kwame Dawes, as part of the Afro Style School (a precursor to The Complete Works) where he challenged the power dynamics of the metaphor and its little sibling the simile as the hegemonic literary device in poetry in English.

[This may have happened around a bonfire—]

(Note, the almost invisible metaphor, that little sibling).

I was very curious about this idea: about how dependent we might be on the image as the foundation of the metaphor, and what would happen if we deprived a poem of this device. Syntactic exposure was one of the things that led me to the *coupling*—thinking about what happens to the lyric if we alter its default settings. How we can fuck about with prose and make music out of it.

*

When my sister told me she had incurable oesophageal cancer I was on the phone in a large garden bordering a park right at the beginning of lockdown and I bent forward as she spoke as if I had been punched.

*

Zak texts a link to a book *Breath: The New Science of a Lost Art*. Its author James Fenton (no, not James Fenton, he's a poet and a critic), James *Nestor* says 'By the law of averages, you will take 670 million breaths in your lifetime.' When I did the Wim Hof breathing with Zak in his room I hated it, I felt like I was going to die. Now I'm thinking about the relationship, etymologically, between the church spire, inspire, conspire, spirit and expire. And the poetic line. How lineation requires us to think about both image and breath. And music, of course, always music.

*

So, how to veer off and get back on track? What does this *zuihitsu* have to do with a diaspora poetics that relates to me, English, Jamaican, Londoner, poet, editor, sociable islander, believer in borderless spaces, the abolition of the nation state, the blur of the mix?

*

> *oh soul,*
>
> i feel
>
> cold and unused to such space as breath and eternity
> around me.

Toi Derricote is a poet whose writing is like a *zuihitsu* even when it's not a zuihitsu because of its intimate tone, because she's not afraid of the elevated lyric, of autobiography, or of being understood; her clear communication is an important act of poetic vulnerability, of resistance. Derricote says joy is an act of resistance. I'm working towards that.

*

Three things I want to write about: My sister. Sugar. Sex. Three things I don't want to write about: Sugar. Sex. Any of my sisters. I often give these lists to my students as freewriting prompts. Did I say that the *Pillow Book* is full of resonant lists? Lists that are in themselves poems.

*

At the funeral by the river I saw five goslings swimming in a
row between two Canada geese in the rain. I took a photo and
hoped there'd be a rainbow over the water but I was distracted
by a handsome osteopath. We chatted about rivers and I men-
tioned writing a *zuihitsu* on a barge in the middle of the
Thames some years back called 'Conversation, With Water'.
This makes me think about reading it on *The Verb* when Jean
'Binta' Breeze was also a guest, and how happy I was that she
liked it, and how rich, how warm her voice was when she said
that. And I mention her here because she has passed, and even
though she wasn't a direct influence on my work, I want her
memory to pass through this piece like a breeze. Actually, she
was on the radio show to talk about her book *The Verandah
Poems* and the verandah is an important indoor/outdoor space
for women in the Caribbean, as it was for Sei Shonagon as a
lady-in-waiting at the Japanese court. It was the place where
gentlemen came a calling and a wooing and Kindle tells me
there are 31 mentions of it in the text. Anyway, digression is
something the *zuihitsu* accommodates as an activity that can
attract knowledge from illogical realms: but now I want to go
back to chatting on the terrace with the handsome pilates
instructor and talking about being on the barge, writing. At the
time I remember noting that being in the middle of the river,
neither north nor south, or both north and south, was a liminal
space I felt comfortable occupying. That being inbetween was
mimetic of my hyphenated English-Jamaican heritage, yet being
in the heart of the river, in London, was conversely iconic and
therefore seemingly whole. I was also interested in the material
and metaphysical properties of water and how we responded to
it as writers and watery beings. This was illustrative of an idea
that I called 'sacred hybridity' which I attempted to coin in my
doctoral thesis. A lot of my work still pursues that line of
enquiry, albeit in oblique ways.

*

It is lovely when is a very Sei Shonagon type of phrase. It is
lovely when I veer off and get back on track. It is lovely when I
discover James Fenton was commissioned to write a poem
about journalists who died in the cause of war reporting to

accompany a large, glass sculpture called 'Breathing'.

*

M—— sends me a link to a lecture on the *zuihitsu* by the Korean-American poet Eugenia Leigh (also of hyphenated identity, note) in which she describes it as 'curated randomness'. No wonder more people are using the form these days, if social media is anything isn't it that? Although algorithmically speaking, it only feels random, when mostly it's highly patterned, shaped, curated.

*

The *zuihitsu* suits the diasporic, in that sense of scattering...

*

In my PhD I used Joy Harjo's books of poems and stories, *A Map to the Next World* and *Conflict Resolution for Holy Beings*, as decolonised theory. Why can't we use poems as theory? As structural intervention?

Kimiko Hahn says of the *zuihitsu*
   The sense of the incomplete, the rough, the random all contribute to suggest the whole subject.

When I came across Joy Harjo's work the first time, in *The Poets' Notebook*, an anthology which included her journal entries, I loved the relaxed voice and the exposed, autobiographical detail in those notebook snippets.

   It is lovely when you get to know a writer through a snippet.
         There is something about that word, snippet.
         We break the line
         at times for emphasis. A line
         is a snippet.

*

It is lovely when I think about how now I'm thinking about a diaspora poetics of illogical realms. How the experience of black and brown bodies is inevitably illogical because they must endure that most illogical thing, racism.

*

At the new apartment where I have an ensuite marble bath-
room, an ensuite marble bathroom I realise I've been manifest-
ing every new moon, I pull *Teiwaz* from the little silk-lined box
that I carry with me here and there. Teiwaz is the Spiritual
Warrior rune. It looks like this: ↑ with its arrow tip pointing
forwards. Spearlike. An ideal symbol for a writer attempting an
ars poetica that is not necessarily that, but which is always that.
Teiwaz counsels patience, perseverance, single-mindedness.

*

In the *Guardian* Roger Robinson says poets 'can translate trauma
into something people can face', and that poems are 'empathy
machines'. I like that he speaks about trauma as presence, as
mutable, that he acknowledges the healing and transformative
possibilities of articulation.

*

Singlemindedness reminds me of Louise Glück's poem 'The
Red Poppy' in *The Wild Iris* (is it really called the *red* poppy?)
and of the clutch of poppies on the roadside I saw last month
in Turkey. So red, and clustered. Vivid on the grey and dusty
concrete of an unpeopled side street. 'The great thing / is not
having / a mind' the delicate, hairy flower proclaims.

(And no, I don't want my mind right now, its implements of
torture, its crucible of delights —)

Now I'm thinking simultaneously, of adjectives, and of mind-
lessness and how poems seek that empty state, Keats' negative
capability—the poem's music being a conduit towards delirium;
and also how I can't help thinking that what the poem needs is
not meditation or *mindfulness* but mindlessness.

                        Wild, abandoned mindlessness.

*

I posted a picture of my little sister's dog, Spike, an Imperial
Shih Tzu, the kind Sei Shonagon might have had. Spike is
waiting patiently in her room at the hospice. The light in that
room was full of sun, the tilt of his head quizzical.

It is lovely when you manage somehow to capture what you've seen or felt, even if only in your own mind, whether it's a photo on a phone, or a poem.

*

Form is
 a freedom and restraint.

> (Don't force it.) Unless you're on deadline —
> An unnecessary joke.

This is the poet's dilemma: when to nurture, when to guide; if we are faithful to a poetics of surprise, of serendipity, then we have to let go of the very thing we need to hold. Not the idea, but yes the idea, and also the vessel, the clay on the wheel. Which is everything. Letting go while holding on. Poetic form asks us to attend to this paradox, it requires discipline. Not the ruler-raps-knuckles stuff of punishment, because discipline is an act more rooted in the conduct of the disciple. I love the long 'i' sound in 'disciple'. How tonally it throws the note, the voice, higher. Its music in ascendance.

*

> *Sunlight, very bright sunlight, flowers, sea, sky, inspire me.*
> *And timelessness, daydreaming, lack of intention—*

Mimi Khalvati lists these as some of the things that inspire her.

*

Over lockdown I read an essay called *In Praise of Shadows* by Juni'chirō Tanizaki.
    It was only 66 pages long but it took me forever to finish.
        Every night I read one page and fell asleep. Its sections were tantalising though:

On construction
The toilet aesthetic
A different course
A novelist's daydreams
On paper, tin and dirt

Bowls of broth
The enigma of shadows
An uncanny silence
Reflections in darkness
Shadows on the stage
The woman of old
Beauty in the dark
A world of shadows
A cool breeze in total darkness
Final grumblings

Bowls of broth. I could keep on saying that. Sometimes we write because we like the sound of something.

The thing I remember most is the section in which I learnt that at the end of the Heian period pubescent boys and girls used to blacken their teeth with soot so the mouth was a gaping hole.

*

Singlemindedness is the exact opposite of what a *ziuhitsu* is, but conversely in order for one to work, you sort of have to pursue that as an ideal.

*

Bernardine Evaristo's creative memoir *Manifesto* is subtitled *On Never Giving Up.*

There have been times when I've almost given up.

There was a time, not long ago, when gatekeepers made lists of words, words that poets couldn't, shouldn't write: shard and mango were on this list. Admittedly I never saw this list, but it existed, apparently. There was a time, not long ago——

It is lovely when
     I leaf through the colour plate section and find a group photo in which I am pictured, along with Bernardine, Patience Agbabi, Malika Booker and Jan Kofi-Tsekpo, amongst others, all dressed in purple, for a publicity shot for *bittersweet: black women's contemporary poetry*
         a book I edited in the last days of the 20th century
         and which had a matching purple cover.

It is lovely when Bernardine wins the Booker Prize, because although this is her singular achievement, we are a community, and she has never given up.

*

My most vivid memory over lockdown was standing outside Barts with a basketful of cold-pressed juices and looking up and the street was grey and the hospital was grey and the windows were grimy and distant and my little sister was locked inside and there wasn't much signal and she was too ill and depressed to answer our texts but she waved, that day, from the window and I waved back from the pavement, and above me the wind whorled and sighed.

*

In his *Book of Runes* Ralph Blum writes that 'the battle of the Spiritual Warrior is with the self'.

*

Another word I like the sound of is *gosling*.

*

When I wrote 'Of Trees & Other Fragments', which is also a *zuihitsu*, I commissioned a friend, Miles Sagnia, who makes complex, driving Detroit techno and other electronica to compose a soundscape for it. Many people are unaware that techno is a creolised form with roots deeply enmeshed in black America, in disco, hi-energy, in hip-hop, as well as UK acid house and rave, German minimalism and prog rock. Somehow, along the way, that history was being slowly erased, which prompted black techno djs to actively address this whitewashing, and which is why I mention it now.

We have to reiterate our imprint to resist erasure—erasure as a tool of white amnesia.

Anyway, Miles sampled recordings of the click-click sounds trees make when they're thirsty. You have to slow the sound right down to make it audible. That poem travels across time and locale, from baobab to oak, to willow, from drought to flood, and is published in *New Daughters of Africa*, a follow-up anthology to an earlier classic edited by Margaret Busby, who also persisted when the literary climate was less favourable.

These name checks could go on, there could be a list, alphabetical, over several pages—

Solmaz Sharif's essay *The Near Transitive Properties of the Political and Poetical: Erasure* speaks to some of these themes with grace and force and subtlety all at once.

I'm conscious that this section is a little nostalgic, and nostalgia is risky; risky, but formally inherent.

A historicity necessary as an act of witness.

*

At the Slade degree show there is only one black artist in the exhibit. This wasn't back in the 90s, or in America: this was last week in London. She has a DJ in her space and he's playing 'Pass the Dutchie', or maybe the original, but I don't really notice that because I'm distracted by the fact that there aren't any other black artists, a situation that's irritating on multiple levels, not least because, as Toni Morrison has said, the 'very serious function of racism is distraction'. When will we be free of this?

*

D—— sends me some Bach Flower remedies in the post:
   Wild Rose, Gentian and Honeysuckle, a cure for
      nostalgia, for those who cannot get over love of a lost one.

*

The artist's name is Maya Simms. Her work depicts black women, often nudes, sometimes amalgams, in some cases pregnant, in others with round, empty bellies; her palette is intense, indigo, terracotta, lush green, Jamaican. My favourite is 'Philanthropist III', a video work depicting 'a molasses pour' over an African mask made out of white sugar.

*

   & all the sugar in Brazil can't bring my little sister back—

*

Is this *zuihitsu* an empathy machine? And why don't I like the word machine? Roger Robinson upgrades William Carlos Williams' definition of a poem as a small or large 'machine made out of words', but empathy or not, why does it have to be a machine?

Xena's note to self, posted on her Mac screen: 'what can AI do that I can't?'

*

Birdsong has no syntax, it has no grammar, it has no sentence structure— if you just allow yourself to listen to it, you don't know what's going to come out.

Mona Arshi's bird poems are buried in the landscape in Norfolk, are in Punjabi.
Little sonic clusters.

Maybe the *zuihitsu* is a bird, a surprising bird, rather than a machine.

*

Breathe.
The answer is breathe. When my little sister stopped breathing we all exhaled, briefly, almost imperceptibly, from relief at her release. I leapt forward to touch her, while her body was still warm. I knew I didn't have long before she got cold and her skin hardened. You know these things only once you have cradled the dead. Once you have encountered the body minus the soul. She always wore factor 50 and her face was virtually unlined. I remember touching her arms, her hands. Saying her name, over and over. Saying her name.

INUA ELLAMS

On time, money and music

I've never cared much for sundials – rudimentary instruments designed to mark the passage of time by following the sun's journey across the sky – but there's a trend in epigraphs and small poems on sundials that I'm taken by. 'Hours fly / flowers die / new days / new ways / pass by' is one of my favourites. 'Let others tell of storms and showers, I'll only count your sunny hours' is another. 'Life is but a shadow', is a double meaning, a play on words, but my favourite is this: 'It is later than you think' – because time and the perception of time differ, and time and its importance also differ.

There's a story about a Chinese-American cellist that beautifully illustrates these differences. It formed the basis of this poem called 'Fuck / Time'.

– x –

Once upon a time / Yo-Yo Ma / travelling through Botswana searching for music / crosses a local shaman singing / into the savannah / He rushes to notate the melody / Please Sing Again he requests / to which the shaman sings something else and explains / to the baffled Yo-Yo Ma / that earlier / clouds had covered the sun and wild antelope grazed in the distance / But the dial of the world had twirled since / The antelopes had cantered into some other future / The clouds had gone / so the song had to change / had to slough off the chains us mortals clasp everything with / even our fluid wrists / The universe in fact is monstrously indifferent to the presence of man / We are small as moth wing fall / in an orchestra broad as galaxies / playing a symphony Time isn't bothered to fathom / It respects no constant and is always moving on

239

For the shaman, the present is more important than the past. He lives in the here and now, and responds to it, whereas Yo-Yo Ma tries to recreate and record the past for some hypothetical use in the future. They are from different worlds.

Every song, every record ever made, is frozen, trapped, packaged passings of time, and the shaman's nature stands in opposition.

The first records ever produced were 12-inch discs made from shellac, where sound vibrations were etched into this brittle plastic. These discs were called 78s because they spun at 78 revolutions per minute, and held 3-4 minuets of sound vibrations. Being able to record and capture the passing of time this way meant songs could be mass produced, and this is when capitalism and industry met music.

In 1949, the record label, RCA, introduced 45rpm records, which were made from vinyl. Like the 78s they held 3-4 minutes of sound but they were more durable, more portable and cheaper than shellacs, which meant 45s could be made for – and marketed to – teenagers. This made 78s obsolete and so infiltrated radio broadcast culture, that for a song to be played on air it had to be delivered on 45s. Much like water takes on the shape if its container, songs took on the dimensions of vinyls and all popular songs roughly became 3mins long. This is when the music industry really exploded, where time constraints, capitalism and song ownership converged to create a trillion dollar market of titans like Tina Turner, The Rolling Stones, Marvin Gaye, Elvis Presley, Tupac Shakur and more, a market in which a star like Yo-Yo Ma could rise. However, when the star Yo-Yo Ma settles, he touches down on a land so divorced from all that culture, not only were songs not recorded, they were constrctured without any consideration to time; the songs made were timeless. In such parts of the world, the phrase 'There is no time like the present' has far deeper resonances.

For most of human history, time differed from culture to culture, world to world. 30,000 years ago, men and woman tracked the earth's rotation – the moon and stars – by carving notches in mammoth tusks. Stonehenge was built to mark the winter and summer solstice, and 4,000 years ago the Nile's flooding in Egypt signalled the new year. Jewish and Christian societies believed time was linear because their holy books dictated the fate of mankind – from creation to rapture – whereas the Incas and Mayans believed time was cyclical and continuous. At one point there were 75 times zones in the United States of America alone. Elsewhere, countries had 13 month calendars, some counted years from when Christ was born, others from when the Prophet Muhammed travelled from Mecca to Medina. Time was hyper-local and tied to how the people experienced nature and religion.

But as humanity marched towards industry when railways, ships, telephones and radios were invented – collapsing time and distance – the various differences caused all kinds of chaos. Commuters would arrive at stations hours after a train had left, there were missed phone calls across countries, and cargo ships weeks late to port... many of those in power were frustrated.

All that began to change in 1884, when a British engineer in Greenwich, London, split the world into 24 time zones and travelled to a conference in Washington DC to convince diplomats to adopt his divisions. A lot of people resented this. There were riots and protests in India that lasted 44 years where locals refused to adopt time as dictated by foreigners. The French adopted a nationwide time, but refused the indignity of complying with the British. Others thought it was an attempt to play God and flatly refused.

But the story of time reform is the story of the record industry, where the forces of capitalism and technology bulldozed its ways into our ways of life. Telegraphs, steamships and railways were harnessed by a particular political vision: a liberal world under European rule, and concepts like Uniformity, Efficiency and Progress reflected Western superiority and European philosophy about human reasoning. Time was developed and imposed accordingly, throughout the periods of colonialisation, to suit their interests, and after missionaries upheld its importance,

241

indigenous populations lost the right to mark their own time.

Opponents of time reform were straight jacketed into a future that was neither necessary, equal or democratic. In such parts of the world, the phrase 'Time is money' has far deeper and perhaps darker resonances.

Time's capitalist colonial culture continues today, enforced by our banking industries, our entertainment and transport industries, permeating so many aspects of life, that those who stand out of it – like a shaman in a savannah – are deemed backward, and those who wish for a slower pace of life are deemed lazy.

What songs might we sing if we were unbound by time? How does time's pressures impact us? What mistakes are made under pressure? If time is money, and money is the root of evil, are we all sinners? Who stands to gain from controlling our smooth efficient futures – and what do we stand to loose? If time was not money, what could it be? How much richer might our worlds be if we took our time to take our time?

Attempting to dramatise these notions, I wrote 'Fuck / Foggy Shuffles', a poem about time-pressures, and the devil himself.

– x –

Because the learner driver is stalled in the middle lane / the mackerel's fin caught in the net / the student 50% sure of the answer / the sunflower root a finger's width from water / Because the high heel is caught in the metal grate / and the blind rat's nose is clogged by fog / I believe the Devil we know / is the work of a Biblical hype man / an MC who strayed far beyond the call / of duty / into the fantastic / conjuring Beelzebub as a hulking goat / a crimson winged demon / a fire-breathing blood sucker / not how he truly appears / coyly / quiet / a flat-capped smiler / of small thumbs and soft words / who comes with options / shuffling through hunkered fog / offering to trade gifts so slight / they feel like a right already earned / clear nasal cavities / a thinner heel / thimbles of water / half a percent more / one smaller fin / and all the time in the world

On a quantum level, all the time in the world does not exist. No time does. Our world, broken into atoms and subatomic particles, is unaffected by time. Though we put molecules together and tear them apart, they are as they have always been – unchanging, monstrously indifferent to the presence of man. Often, I imagine a needle on a vinyl record scratching away at its groves, wearing the melodies down as the smallest plastic molecules – the tinniest parts of songs – break and splinter away. I often imagine this as an act of rebellion against the record industry, against time and money, and rap music is the sound of rebellion.

The world as it is today is the result of vast inequalities, formed and compounded over generations. These inequalities resulted in the suffering, servitude and deaths of millions, caused by a small inbred, greedy elite in the quest for world domination, all facilitated by global insurance and banking groups.

The Black African descendants, those who suffered the most, found themselves crammed into crumbling neighborhoods in New York City in the 1970s. After 400 years of slavery in America, they harbored a healthy distrust of governments and an innate understanding that corporate cultures do not best serve the interests of the individual. Many were locked out of high-paying jobs and forced into demeaning hard labor that benefited the white supremacist states.

Despite the depravation, like a shaman singing into a savannah, their growing self-consciousness, self-worth, and self-pride, needed a form of expression. They could not afford musical instruments or recording equipment, so picked up old discarded 78s and 45s, pressed play, and when they heard breakbeats, quieter times between melodic instrumentation – space enough to speak and be heard – they would stop the record and drag it backwards, scratching plastic molecules away as they did, literally reversing the passing of time, then release it into their present, over and over again, speaking into the here and now, about their here and now.

In block parties and social gatherings, the masters of such musical ceremonies, the MCs, would freestyle – making up rhyming stories in real time like the shaman in the savannah. They spoke over hard, eviscerating beats which perfectly represented the harsh capitalist march towards profit and oblivion that had bulldozed its way into their lives, and the lives of their ancestors. And as soon as they could record these sonic experiments, those early rap artists, those MCs, would spread positive messages and tell stories connecting their American-ness to their African-ness – their present selves to their historic past – that their future selves might better understand their lives and lineages. It must have felt like science-fiction, like Afro-futurism, all that alchemy and plastic, savannah-grass and song, converging in basements of falling buildings.

Much has changed since those early days of hip hop. Time, money and capitalism cut through those early pure intentions. In the quests for larger markets and profits, record labels pushed rappers and MCs to glorify the same relentless quests for profit and the same types of violence that had destroyed their ancestors and ancestral lands.

What if a rapper could step out of time to become a lord of time? What if such an MC, such a musician could divorce time from money, and pulse – as if a bolt of lightning – through time, space and telegraph poles, appearing everywhere and nowhere? What if rather than a flat-capped smiler / of small thumbs and soft words, an MC appeared at the nick of time, generous, positive and benevolent? Meditating on time, money and music, I wrote 'Fuck / Drums', this final poem, in which such a hero rises from the African continent, comes at us through 45s and 78 inch records, battling through time, to arrive in the here and now.

– x –

When I claim hip hop as afrofuturist expressionism / Exhibit A is the ancient West African Sankofa symbol / of a bird walking forward whilst looking back / like a rapper following a beat's forward progression / whilst recalling lyrics / anticipating the future whilst conjuring the past / and the rapper is the gasp of stillness between / the ghost in the time machine / Say time is marked by drums / and each strike stakes its signature / the rapper's task is to find within its solid lines / equilibrium / to fuck up the drum's ubiquitous significance by rhyming / on / within / or off its beat / to render it inaudible / invisible / fluid as if a bird dancing through a stave of barbed wires / its wings aflutter / like a tongue between gritted teeth / twirling urban narratives into timeless myth / shit / it's the stuff of science fiction / ain't it / each rapper's mouth a Quantum realm / a Tardis / a Delorean / and the beat maker a mad scientist / Y'all don't see how all electricity is Sango's lightning pulse / that Dr Emmet Brown is Grand Master Flash in disguise / and Andre 3000 is the greatest Time Lord / who grabbed a mic / to spit

ACKNOWLEDGEMENTS

Acknowledgements are due to the following publications in which these poems are first published, with permission granted by the authors before the collections noted were published, or with the permission of the publishers specified here where copyright agreements require this.

Raymond Antrobus: 'The Perseverance' was first published in *The Perseverance* (Penned in the Margins, 2018) and 'Horror Scene as Black English Royal (Captioned)' in *All the Names Given* (Picador, 2021).

Mona Arshi: 'Yellows' was published in *Poetry London*, 'February' in *INQUE*, and 'Arrivals', '*from* My Little Sequence of Ugliness' and '*from* The Book of Hurts' in *bath magg*.

Jay Bernard: 'Clearing' from Surge (Chatto & Windus, 2019), by permission of Penguin Random House; 'Manifesto', from *The Poetry Review*, 107:3, Autumn 2017, by permission of the author and The Poetry Society.

Victoria Adukwei Bulley: three poems first published in *Quiet* (Faber & Faber, 2022).

Kayo Chingonyi: 'Kumukanda' and 'The Colour of James Brown's Scream' from *Kumukanda* (Chatto & Windus, 2017) and 'Nyaminyami: 'water can crash and water can flow' and 'Nyaminyami: epilogue' from *A Blood Condition* (Chatto & Windus, 2022), by permission of Penguin Random House.

Rishi Dastidar: 'The Brexit Book of the Dead' and 'Neptune's concrete crash helmet' from *Neptune's Projects* (Nine Arches Press, 2023).

Edward Doegar: 'After After Remainder' appeared in *The Poetry Review*.

Will Harris: 'In June, outrageous stood the flagons...' and 'Take the origin of banal...' are from *Brother Poem* (Granta Poetry, 2023).

Ian Humphreys: 'the grasshopper warbler's song' was published in *The Poetry Review* and 'The wood warbler's song' in *The Rialto*, and both poems in *Tormentil* (Nine Arches Press, 2023). 'Swifts and the Awakening City' was originally written for the BBC Arts poetry film project *Dancing the Distance* (Contains Strong Language, 2021).

Adam Lowe: 'Gingerella's Date', 'Elegy for the Latter-Day Teen Wilderness Years' and 'Reynardine for Red' from *Patterflash* (Peepal Tree Press, 2023).

Mir Mahfuz Ali: 'My Salma' from *Midnight, Dhaka* (Seren Books, 2014).

Shazea Quraishi: 'The Taxidermist attends to her work' from *The Glimmer* (Bloodaxe Books, 2022).

Roger Robinson: 'Halibun for the Onlookers' and 'Woke' from *A Portable Paradise* (Peepal Tree Press, 2019).

Yomi Ṣode: 'The Exhibition 2.0' and 'An Ode to Bruv, Ting, Fam and, on Occasion, Cuz & My Man' were published in *Manorism* (Penguin Books, 2022).

Degna Stone: 'Proof of life on earth' was published by the Museum of Colour. 'over {prep., adv}' was published in *More Fiya: a New Collection of Black British Poetry*, ed. Kayo Chingonyi (Canongate, 2022) and in Degna Stone's collection *Proof of Life on Earth* (Nine Arches Press, 2022).

Jennifer Lee Tsai: 'About Chinese Women' was published in *The White Review*.